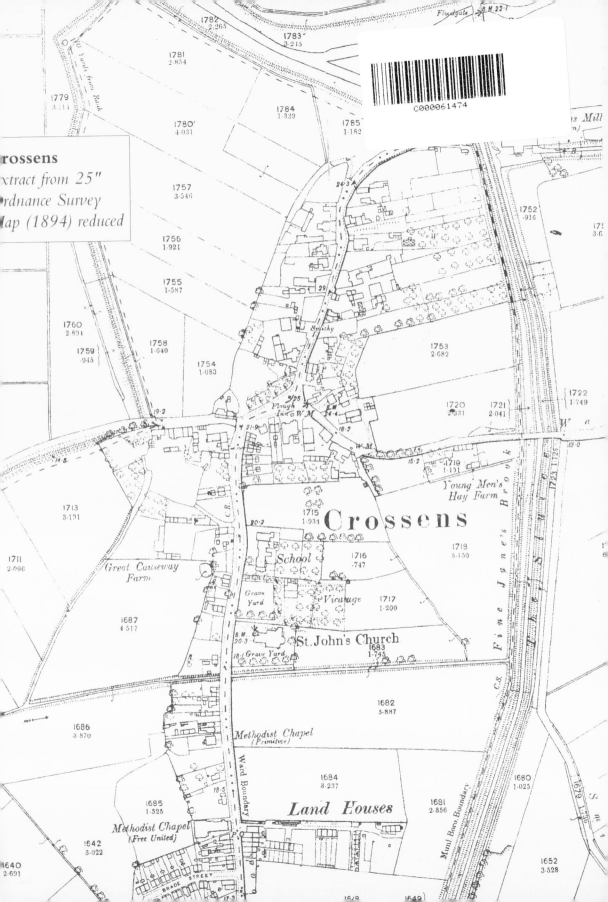

Crossens

*Extract from 25"
Ordnance Survey
Map (1894) reduced*

Crossens

School

Grave
Yard

Vicarage

St. John's Church

Grave Yard

Methodist Chapel
(Primitive)

Land Houses

Methodist Chapel
(Free United)

Great Causeway
Farm

Young Men's
Hay Farm

Plough
Inn

Smithy

BRADE STREET

Crossens

Southport's Cinderella Suburb

Crossens Pool c. 1894

Crossens

Southport's Cinderella Suburb

Harry Foster

Birkdale and Ainsdale Historical Research Society

ISBN 0 9510905 6 9

A Limited Edition of 1,000 Books published by
The Birkdale and Ainsdale Historical Research Society
in 2002

Typeset in 12 on 14 point Bembo
and printed in Great Britain by
Hughes & Company
Kempsey, Worcestershire, England

Contents

Illustrations   vii

Preface   x

CHAPTER ONE   – *The Early Years: A Farming Hamlet*   1

CHAPTER TWO   – *An Isolated Agricultural Village 1800-1875*   19

CHAPTER THREE   – *Incorporation and the Bulpit Years*
                   1875-1904   49

CHAPTER FOUR   – *The Vulcan Fires Crossens 1904-1945*   79

CHAPTER FIVE   – *Farms and Factories Give Way to Housing*
                   1945-2000   115

CHAPTER SIX   – *Crossens: Some Conclusions*   136

Sources   138

Index of Names   141

Index of Subjects   145

Birkdale and Ainsdale Historical Research Society

Crossens: Southport's Cinderella Suburb is the ninth in the Society's series of publications and shares the aims of its predecessors – to find new material about the district and then present it in a manner which will bring enjoyment and pleasure to readers. Several of our previous publications are now out of print and have become scarce, collectable items. All our new books are limited editions. Society members are presently engaged in projects which should result in several further publications. We are grateful to have access to any material that relates to the Southport area.

Sylvia Harrop
Publications Editor

Previous Publications

Sylvia Harrop, *Old Birkdale and Ainsdale: Life on the south-west Lancashire Coast 1600–1851*, B. & A.H.R.S. (1985).★

Peggy Ormrod, *Birkdale and Ainsdale Past and Present: The 1845 tithe map superimposed on a modern street plan*, B. & A.H.R.S. (1987).

Sylvia Harrop (ed.), *Families and Cottages of Old Birkdale and Ainsdale*, Carnegie Publishing (1992).

Harry Foster, *New Birkdale: The Growth of a Lancashire Seaside Suburb 1850–1912*, Alan Sutton Publishing (1995).★

Harry Foster, *Southport: A Pictorial History*, Phillimore (1995).

Harry Foster, *Links Along the Line: The Story of the Development of Golf Between Liverpool and Southport*, B. & A.H.R.S. (1996).★

Harry Foster, *Don E Want Ony Srimps? The Story of the Fishermen of Southport and North Meols*, B. & A.H.R.S. (1998).

Harry Foster, *New Ainsdale: The Struggle of a Seaside Suburb 1850-2000*, B. & A.H.R.S. (2000).

★ New copies of these books are no longer available in shops.

Further details of the Society's publications from:
Mrs. P. M. Perrins,
Hon. Secretary,
Birkdale and Ainsdale Historical Research Society,
20 Blundell Drive, Birkdale,
Southport, PR8 4RG.

Illustrations

FRONTISPIECE: Crossens Pool c.1894

CHAPTER ONE – *The Early Years: A Farming Hamlet*

1 The Plantation	2
2 An extract of Yates' Map 1786	3
3 One of Crossens' glacial erratics	4
4 Manorial village of North Meols 1736	6
5 St Cuthbert's Church 1739	8
6 Cottages with two storeys	10
7 Pair of thatched cottages	11
8 A pebble wall	12
9 An extract of Bankes' Map 1736	13
10 Memorial to Thomas Fleetwood in St. Cuthbert's Church	14
11 An eel spearer	15
12 Bulpit and the logboat in Water Lane 1899	16
13 The logboat in the Botanic Gardens Museum c. 1905	16
14 The 'Fylde' at Hesketh Bank	16

CHAPTER TWO – *An Isolated Agricultural Village 1800-1875*

15 A pair of cottages with a slate roof and brick walls	20
16 Articles of the Cow Club 1858	24
17 A pig being slaughtered	25
18 A labourer working on a sea-bank	26
19 Hauling sods over the saltings on a sledge	26
20 Grass plantings on the saltings	26
21 Reaping, raking and sheaf binding	28
22 Potato picking	28
23 The pumping station and mill	30
24 Horse waiting outside Moss Lane smithy	31
25 John Tomlinson, a Scarisbrick Estate gamekeeper	35
26 Vaulting a drainage ditch	36
27 A snipe catcher	36
28 Boys outside the old school	40
29 Primitive Methodist Chapel, Rufford Road	43
30 The principal roads in the Township of North Meols 1835	45

CHAPTER THREE – *Incorporation and the Bulpit Years 1875-1904*

31 The Reverend William Bulpit with two of his daughters   52

32 Charles Scarisbrick   53

33 A Rufford Road cottage opposite to Brook Street   54

34 Tomlinson's builder's yard from a window of The Plough   55

35 A road gang and steamroller in Crossens   57

36 Scavenger and cart alongside Barton's Farm, Water Lane   57

37 The small cramped terraced houses of 'The Fold'   58

38 The rebuilt Plough Hotel and the houses which replaced 'The Fold'   58

39 New modest, but solidly built, semi-detached houses in Rufford Road   59

40 Building in Rufford Road   60

41 'Mayfield', 235 Rufford Road   61

42 The 'Scarisbrick bungalows' at the junction of Rufford Road and Banks Road   61

43 St. John's Church without the tower   62

44 William Leatherbarrow, headmaster of St. John's School   63

45 St. John's – Harvest Festival decorations c.1895   64

46 Guests at a church function   64

47 Boys ducking in a trough at Plough Farm   65

48 The Scarisbrick mausoleum dominated the churchyard   66

49 The United Methodist Chapel and school room   67

50 A village funeral passes down Rufford Road   67

51 A procession to mark Queen Victoria's Diamond Jubilee 1897   68

52 Water from the Mere being pumped into Crossens Pool   70

53 Reaping by machine   70

54 Loading a four-wheeled wagon   70

55 J. Ball's outfit   71

56 A steam engine driving a threshing machine   71

57 Scarisbrick gamekeepers   72

58 Netting rabbits in a ditch bank on the Mere   73

59 Southport Royal Caledonian Curling Club c.1895   73

60 Curling on a frozen field alongside Water Lane   74

61 Shrimp 'putters'   75

62 Boatyard at Crossens Pool c.1900   76

CHAPTER FOUR – *The Vulcan Fires Crossens 1904-1945*

63 Drawing of the new Vulcan factory 1906   81

64 Enlarged Vulcan works, post 1911   82

65 Vulcan power house and the clock tower   83

66 Vulcan machine shop   83

67 Vulcan radiator mascot   84

68 Vulcan cars came in all shapes and sizes   85

69 Aeroplane manufacture at Vulcan   86

70 Vulcan football team   87

71 Celebrating the production of lorry chassis no. 1,000 in 1920   88

72 The Vulcan Standard Saloon 1925   90

73 Building Vulcan bus bodies   91

74 A Crossens washerwoman   92

75 An Ideal Laundry delivery van   93

76 Hawking farm produce outside The Plough   95

77 Shallow-draught fishing boats   96

78 Rufford Road – the new centre of the village   97

79 198 Rufford Road – the police office   98

80 Newly-built council houses in North Road   100

81 Ribble Avenue   100

82 Elizabeth Tomlinson talking to a distinguished looking visitor outside her shop   101

83 Jane Tomlinson poses for her brother's camera   102

84 Cottage at the corner of Rufford Road and Dock Lane   103

85 The Festival Queen on her horse 1907   106

86 Maypole dancers 1906   107

87 Village wedding 1913   107

88 Stalls had to be manned 1907   108

89 Tail-plane of a Junkers 88 bomber   111

CHAPTER FIVE – *Farms and Factories Give Way to Housing 1945-2000*

90 New pumping station c.1963   116

91 Bank End sewerage works   117

92 Brockhouse's Corgi motor cycle   119

93 Mullard's factory extensions c.1971   120

94 Crossens station 1964   122

95 Two factory units on the Fylde Road fields c.1965   123

96 The Causeway Farm estate   124

97 Preparing the roads on the Drewitt Crescent site   126

98 Building on the Skipton Avenue/Harrogate Way site 1969   126

99 Land for the builders c.1969   128

100 Crossens Nursery School 2000   132

101 Crossens Library 2000   132

102 St. John's Air Scouts   133

CHAPTER SIX – *Crossens: Some Conclusions*

TAILPIECE: 'A Rufford Road Resident'   137

ENDPAPERS

Front Extract from O.S. Map 1848. Extract from O.S. Map 1894

Rear Extract from O.S. Map 1911. Extract from O.S. Map 1929

Preface

Unlike Birkdale and Ainsdale, Crossens was never an administratively independent area. Nevertheless it did have an identity of its own and, as in the neighbouring communities of Marshside and Banks, there was a fierce local pride. I chose to write the story of Crossens because it is distinctively different from that of the rest of the town, but ironically it is these differences which made it an integral, if unique, part of developing Southport.

As always a great debt is owed for the courteous and very professional assistance that is available from local libraries and record offices. I would particularly like to thank Andrew Farthing, the Local History Librarian, and the other members of staff of the Southport Reference Library, Joanna Denton, for help at the Botanic Gardens Museum, and staff at the Liverpool and Lancashire Record Offices. The collections of the Public Record Office and The National Society have also been consulted. Many local residents have been generous in sharing their knowledge of Crossens and in making photographs available. They include: David Albert, Bob Abram, John Ball, Stan Ball, Alan Bond, Keith Bond, Terence Burgess, John Cotterall, Audrey Coney, Brian Garston, Dave Gregson, Gilbert Hall, Jack Harris, Bill Howard, Peter Howard, Peter Jelley, Peter Lynch, Peggy Ormrod, B. Parker, Tom Rimmer, Kath Robinson, Elizabeth Shorrock, Mrs. Slater, Brian Street, Ron Taylor, and Geoff Wright. Alan Reid Whittaker has again been generous with his time and expertise in copying photographs and slides; Ian McDowall helped me to make prints from the glass negatives; whilst Chris Driver made computer enhancements of some particularly poor images. Artwork is by my son David.

I will always be grateful for the guidance that I received in shaping my approach to local history from Bill Marsden. Finally, thanks are due to my wife Thelma and to members of the Birkdale and Ainsdale Historical Research Society, especially Sylvia Harrop, the Society's Publications Editor, and Pat Perrins, the Secretary. Without the support of this trinity, I would not have produced a single book.

Harry Foster

CHAPTER ONE

The Early Years:
A Farming Hamlet

In remote times Crossens consisted of a small collection of boulder huts erected on a sand mound at the outlet of Martin Mere.
W.T. Bulpit - Vicar of Crossens 1878-1904

O F ALL THE ancient settlements of the parish of North Meols, Crossens appears to have the most obvious etymology. It was a name that attracted many variations in spelling. In the North Meols parish registers for the years 1594 to 1731 there are no fewer than thirteen. Early written forms include 'Crossenes' and 'Crosnes'. This led both Bulpit[1] (a vicar of Crossens and an enthusiastic antiquarian) and Bailey[2] (the author of Southport's most comprehensive and authoritative local history) to suggest that it is derived from the compound of 'Cross-ness' based upon 'the ness (or headland) with the cross'. Their theory was that it indicated a cross set up as a guide for travellers, probably associated with a monastic hospice or lodging-house. Farrer (the principal authority on the early history of North Meols) notes that the name appears in the Viking *Landnama-bok* as 'Krossa-nes', and '… clearly refers to a point, or ness, where stood a cross.'[3] Sadly there is no archaeological, or even direct historical, evidence to confirm the existence of a Crossens cross. Nevertheless, on the strength of its name alone, the likelihood that there was some kind of a cross at Crossens appears to be very strong. Its possible location was the open area of high ground, in front of what is now the Plough Hotel *(Fig. 1)*. This public space became known as 'The Plantation', and Bulpit identified it as having been the venue for cockfighting and bear baiting;[4] whilst Edward Baines, writing in the 1830s, noted that bull baits had frequently been one of the Christmas sports.[5]

An alternative derivation for the name was 'Cross Sands' indicating a Ribble crossing from the Fylde to Crossens. Bulpit and Farrer rejected this

1

Fig. 1. The Plantation. Looking down Banks Road, the high ground on which the early hamlet developed. The ornate three-burner gas lamp was said to be on the site of the old Maypole and possibly the cross

view; nevertheless, others have speculated that in medieval times travellers did ford the Ribble at this point. Ashton, in his heavily geographical book *The Evolution of a Coast-Line,* suggests that there was a Ribble crossing between Freckleton Naze on the Fylde and a point about a mile to the north of Banks.[6] Thompson Watkin, an early authority on Roman Lancashire, suggested that a Roman fort might once have guarded a crossing from Freckleton.[7] Bulpit offered evidence of Roman influence, as far west as Crossens, by repeating Thomas Brookfield's admission that at some time prior to 1860, he had discovered a number of silver sepulchral urns and coins from the time of Vespasian.[8] Brookfield lived in a cottage on reclaimed land outside the old sea-wall; and he later told Bulpit that he found the urns, '... ranged like mugs on a buttery shelf', whilst cultivating his plot. He claimed that the landowner, Charles Scarisbrick, had the urns taken to Scarisbrick Hall, but Brookfield had apparently concealed his find of coins. When some later turned up in the district, they were traced back to him. Although details of this find were shrouded in secrecy, rumours about it were common. A 1911 Ordnance Survey map revealed a precise site for the cache, and dated the find as 1840 *(see rear endpaper).*

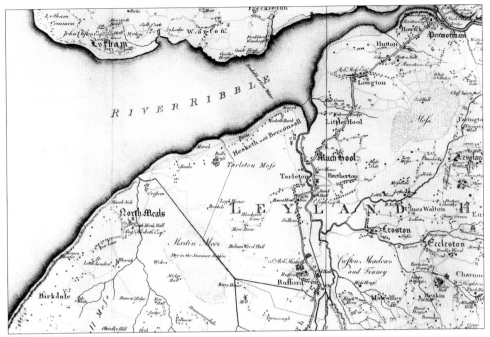

Fig. 2. An extract of Yates' Map 1786

There was certainly a Ribble crossing between Freckleton Naze and Hesketh Bank, up-river from Crossens, by the seventeenth century. It was here during the Civil War that, after defeat at Marston Moor in 1644, some 2,000 Royalist (Cavalier) cavalry escaped their Parliamentary (Roundhead) pursuers by fording the river. Faced by a further Parliamentary force at Hesketh Bank, the Royalists turned west and '... marched up to the Mealles'.[9] Based on the evidence of musket balls and small calibre canon balls found during building excavations in Brade Street and Land Lane, Bulpit concluded that this force fought a skirmish in Crossens.[10] There is no documentary evidence to support this claim, but the Royalist force was brought to action a few days later near Ormskirk and routed.

The track of this ancient ford of the Ribble is clearly marked on the Fearon and Eyes 1736 survey of the estuary, and again on Yates' map of 1786 *(Fig. 2)*. An earlier map of 1712, by Thomas Steer the dock engineer at Liverpool, indicates its location with a drawing of a horse pulling a cart across the river. Edward Baines in his *History of Lancashire*, published in 1836, noted that the Ribble was three miles wide '... from Hesketh Bank to the Guide's House on Freckleton Marsh' and was '... fordable under the conduct of a guide appointed for the purpose.'[11] Evidence of the use of the crossing can be found in several contemporary accounts. In 1772 Thomas Langton, a flax merchant

3

Fig. 3. One of Crossens' glacial erratics. This boulder now stands opposite to the pumping station, where it was unearthed in 1959

of Kirkham, arranged a crossing for his sons returning from school in Liverpool.[12] Later in 1835, the Rev. Charles Hesketh, the newly appointed rector of North Meols, '... crossed the Ribble at Hesketh Bank Ford in the carriage and gig and carts full of furniture and livestock ... The cart with the live creatures, namely pigs, dogs, cats and poultry, stuck in the bed of the river, but was got out in time.'[13] The inscription on the gravestone of James Blundell in Old Becconsall churchyard emphasises the treacherous nature of the Ribble estuary:

> Often times I've crossed the sands
> And through the Ribble deep
> But I was found in Astland drowned
> It was God's will it should be so
> Some way or other all must go

The estuary still claims occasional victims, even from amongst the ranks of experienced wildfowlers. Between 1965 and 1968 there were as many as eleven deaths on the mudflats. Nevertheless, a ford of the Ribble from Crossens to the Fylde on foot cannot be discounted. In 1935, Peter (Pluck) Wright, a Marshside fisherman, conducted a journalist on such a crossing.[14]

An ancient settlement, Crossens developed on a boulder clay knoll of high ground. It was an island, rising above the tide and winter floods, '... where

4

hay and corn could be stacked without fear of damage.'[15] It was here that the early farms were clustered *(see front endpaper)*. The road through Crossens was some twelve feet above the level of the beach. A combination of later subsidence of the land and accretion on the beach has partially levelled out this area, although there is still a gradient (brew) on all the roads approaching the crest of the knoll, on Banks Road. Local evidence of glacial action can be seen in the form of the five-and-a-half ton boulder, which was found some seventeen feet deep during the excavations for the new pumping stationhouse in 1959 *(Fig. 3)*. Two further striated stones were found when St. John's Church was being built in 1836. Both of these stones can now be seen in the churchyard; one is of Shap granite, whilst the other is limestone. Situated at the mouth of the Ribble estuary, the sand at Crossens was tidal alluvium brought down by the river, rather than the blown sand of the rest of the North Meols coast. A feature of the beach at Crossens was an extensive bed of pebbles, which was later covered by silt. Bulpit suggested that '… in remote times Crossens consisted of a small collection of boulder huts erected on a mound at the outlet of Martin Mere.'[16]

Inland, between Crossens and Rufford, lay Martin Mere, south-west Lancashire's vast seasonal lake of legend. It was a shallow lake, nowhere deeper that twelve feet, even in its wettest phases, and in summer it would be much reduced in size and depth. The main outflow was into the Ribble through Tarleton, although a map presented at an eighteenth-century court case showed that it also regularly drained into The Pool at Churchtown *(Fig. 4)*.[17] In addition it seems that when the level of the Mere rose very high, there was a further occasional outlet at Crossens, which was normally blocked by alluvium.

Crossens was one of the scattered hamlets of North Meols *(see Fig. 2)*. In medieval times the area had monastic connections; most famously it was the site of the salt-pit of Cistercian Sawley Abbey, in the Ribble Valley. Salt, an important preservative and condiment, was obtained from seawater. Tidal water was channelled onto the sand in shallow lagoon-like ponds and allowed to evaporate. The salt was then dissolved out of the sand and the salt boiled out of the brine in a lead pan over a fire, burning turf from the nearby moss. The field name Pyttes (Salt Pit) dates from this time. The mid-nineteenth-century *North Meols tithe map and award* included Salthouse Fields and Salthouse Moss, and it is assumed that the ponds were located in the vicinity of the former railway bridge linking Bankfield Lane and Rufford Road. A similar operation for the extraction of salt was to be found further north on the Fylde.

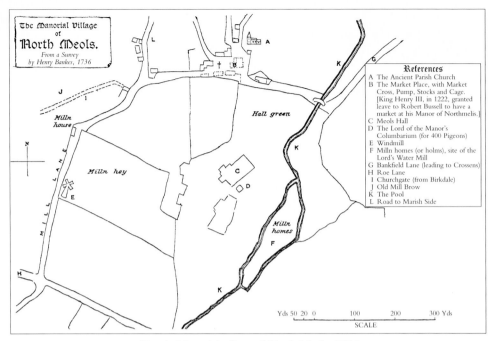

The Manorial Village of North Meols.
From a Survey by Henry Bankes, 1736

References
A The Ancient Parish Church
B The Market Place, with Market Cross, Pump, Stocks and Cage. [King Henry III, in 1222, granted leave to Robert Bussell to have a market at his Manor of Northmelis.]
C Meols Hall
D The Lord of the Manor's Columbarium (for 400 Pigeons)
E Windmill
F Milln homes (or holms), site of the Lord's Water Mill
G Bankfield Lane (leading to Crossens)
H Roe Lane
I Churchgate (from Birkdale)
J Old Mill Brow
K The Pool
L Road to Marish Side

Yds 50 20 0   100   200   300 Yds
SCALE

Fig. 4. Manorial village of North Meols 1736

In an arrangement with Evesham Abbey, monks from Penwortham held North Meols church and had land, a grange and a tithe barn at Crossens. According to Bulpit, these were on what later became Rectory Farm in Banks Road, the grange being at the corner of Banks Road and Skipton Road, with the tithe barn nearby. The monks were also responsible for installing the priest at North Meols and building a rectory for him at Crossens. This also was on the Town Causeway, now Banks Road, the high ground around which the early development of the hamlet took place. This parsonage house was to provide Crossens with its most lurid historical tale. A late fourteenth-century parson, John de Lyverpull, was reputed to be a wealthy man. A gang of villains, led by a Roger de Blyth of Lathom, broke into the house and, in an attempt to get the parson to reveal where he kept his valuables, they poured water into his mouth through a pipe. The thieves escaped with about twenty pounds, jewels and other possessions. The alleged culprits were brought to trial at the Lancaster Sessions in 1400, but surprisingly were acquitted.[18] It appears that the explanation for this perverse verdict might have owed more to politics than to justice.

As late as in Elizabethan days, it is claimed that St. Cuthbert's, the ancient parish church of North Meols, stood on a sandy elevation just above high water mark at Churchtown, on the south side of North Meols Bay.[19] The road to the north and the Ribble crossing curved inland around North Meols Bay along the line of Bankfield Lane and on through Crossens. These areas now seem remote from the sea, but accounts suggest that the sea washed against the sand-hill mound on which St. Cuthbert's was built and up to the line of Bankfield Lane. This, as the name suggests, was on the crest of an old sea-wall embankment, which had been built by the monks in the thirteenth century. Thus, until comparatively recent times, Crossens was separated from Churchtown by the curve of North Meols Bay. Early maps of Lancashire, such as Bowen's, first published in 1752, show this bay. Bagley judged that this map was '... unusually informative about the waters off the Lancashire coast', adding that the coastline had been '... delineated ... with some care.'[20] These accounts are supported by archaeological evidence. Excavations in 1903 revealed what was taken to be the remains of a quay at Churchtown; whilst beds of shells and the remnants of wrecks also pointed to the area's seaside past. As new sea-banks were built and more land reclaimed, the outlet of the Otter Pool Stream (later the Old Pool and referred to by Bulpit as Meols River), that ran through the grounds of Meols Hall, was trained (see Fig. 4). Known as the New Pool (it now forms the lake of the Botanic Gardens) the water course flowed north to Crossens, where it joined the sea at a small creek, which was roughly in the vicinity of the present pumping station. Farrer quotes a deed of 1550 identifying a 'mussel skeyre' in this area of Crossens. It is described as a '... ditch flowing into the sea, below the level of ordinary tides, where mussels were cultivated.'[21] Bulpit wrote of a 'mussel skaur'; whilst others refer to such beds as 'skeers'.

The rectory was built alongside the creek at Crossens. After the houses of the two lords of the manor, this was the largest house in North Meols. We are told that the rector had a boat shed and a boat, which he used to travel to St. Cuthbert's (Fig. 5).[22] Interestingly, the very detailed list of the chattels of one rector, Matthew French, who died in 1614, did not include a boat.[23] It seems that this creek was one of the points at which the overflow from Martin Mere periodically found its way to the sea. The area around the creek was known as Fiddler's Ferry, and is still so marked on Ordnance Survey maps. Charles Abram, a local fisherman and self-styled 'amateur historian', claimed that there was a small long-forgotten and now demolished hamlet, immediately beyond the creek, called Bayman's Loan (Lane). There was a ferry across the creek and big tides were known to put out the fires in the creek-side cottages. According to Abram, several of the old Crossens families – the Bonds, Brookfields,

Fig. 5. St. Cuthbert's Church 1739. An engraving of the ancient parish church as it appeared shortly after a rebuilding

Wrights and Wareings – lived there. His account appears to be based on oral folk memories.[24] Genealogical research has perhaps given a more accurate picture of Crossens' longest established families. Aughton (the best-informed family historian amongst the chroniclers of North Meols' story) identifies Bond, along with Ball, as probably '… the oldest families still extant in North Meols parish.'[25] Bulpit names several Bonds of Crossens, including Nicholas Bonnde '… who in 1565 owned the ship Bartholomew, one of the twelve biggest which sailed out of Liverpool.' He went on to state that the Bonds had a ship-building yard at Crossens.[26] Liverpool had a population of barely 1,000 at this time. Evidence from the Bartholomew's charters show that Bonnde, first as master and then as the owner, was engaged in coastal trade, as were most of the ships sailing out of Liverpool. Water transport was the most economical way of moving bulky materials. In 1563 and again in 1565, the Bartholomew discharged cargoes of iron and salt at Hesketh Bank.[27]

The alluvial soil of Crossens was some of the most fertile in the sandy North Meols parish, and further potential agricultural land was obtained as new turf sea-banks enclosed former marsh and beach. There were a number of substantial farms in Crossens, which were held by yeoman families. Brekleyhey was one of the fields of Breakill's Land, near Martin Mere. This was the farm of the Breakhell family (a name which is also variously spelt as Breakyll, Brekyll, Breakhill, and Brekhill). The Copelands had a farm opposite the old rectory; the Blevins held land around New Lane; the Wrights were another farming family; whilst Thomas Rymer reclaimed part of the 200-acre Crossens Moss. Parish records reveal that at least one trade, other than those related to agriculture, was practised in Crossens. In 1716 Richard Such, a pauper boy, was apprenticed to a tailor – George Boond (Bond) of Crossens.[28] This evidence does not prove that all Boond's time was given to tailoring; my great-great-grandfather was a tailor living in Moss Lane, but he also farmed.

Returns for the hearth tax in 1666 give a list of twenty-four householders in Crossens: three Rymers and a Rimer, two Wrights, two Tomasons, a Blevin and a Blevine, and single Allonson, Bannester, Blundell, Bond, Bradshaw, Breakell, Copeland, Haworth, Heaworth, Liniker, Matthews, Scarisbrick, Such, and Wignall families.[29] The total population was only 132. Nevertheless, Bishop Gastrell, who compiled a list of the scattered hamlets of the parish of North Meols between 1720 and 1725, judged Crossens to be second only to Churchtown in both size and importance.[30] In 1690 Thomas Blevin, a Crossens farmer, demonstrated his wealth by giving twenty pounds to the North Meols Grammar School.[31]

Bulpit suggests that to serve this farming community in Crossens there was both a limekiln, where later the ivy-clad Liverpool House stood, at the corner of Rufford Road and North Road; and a windmill, opposite to Pool Street. Clare wrote that: 'The sea washed close to where Crossens church now stands … a windmill was erected on the shore … which was known as the Asshurst Mill. The stretch of land seaward was marsh.'[32] Farrer, who wrote of 'Asshehurste Mylle', had earlier identified this windmill.[33] The view that there had been a mill on this site was reinforced by the old name for the area – 'Mill Brow'.

Crossens certainly had an inn – The Plough – although Wright, an authority on early Southport hostelries, tells us that it was originally called 'The Letter and Board'.[34] It was a little further east, down Water Lane, than the existing late nineteenth-century building (see front endpaper). In 1776, 'Duke' William Sutton, the supposed founder of Southport, married Jane Gregson, the innkeeper's daughter.

Normally the cottages of North Meols were constructed with timber cruck frames and walls of wattle and daub. A bent or split tree trunk in the shape of a letter 'A' formed the cruck. The crucks were the main support for the roof.

Fig. 6. Cottages with two storeys. This mix of property was in Banks Road, the heart of the old hamlet

Long buildings needed more support than would have been offered by the crucks in the two end walls. Additional crucks could be added and the spaces between them were called bays. The number of bays it had described a building. Farmhouses would normally have more than one bay. An insurance claim made by Peter Rymer, following a fire in 1749, showed that his building had four bays and was valued at £82-10s (£82.50);[35] whilst a lease granted by Robert Hesketh to Richard Wright in 1754 was for a farm of five bays, with a further two bays for the outhouse.[36] Some farms were built with a full second storey, or had one added *(Fig. 6)*.

Wooden pegs secured the rough-hewn timbers of the house frames. The walls were made from daub on a lattice of twigs or light timber. Crossens was the only part of North Meols with an abundant supply of clay for the daub; elsewhere local mud had to be stiffened with horsehair and cow dung. Windows were small making the cottages dark inside. Deep thatch on the roofs provided superb, all the year round, insulation – warm in winter, cool in summer. Following the draining of much of the Mere, reed thatch was frequently replaced by wheat straw *(Fig. 7)*. Reed thatch could last for up to three times longer. An unusual feature in Crossens was that some of the early dwellings were built out of local boulders. Robert Brookfield, whose family had lived in the cottages by the old

Three Pools Bridge for over 200 years, wrote of the large boulders, or pebbles, being plentiful in the red glacial boulder clay.[37] Percy Howard, who was born in Crossens in 1890, spoke of pebbles being extracted from a quarry in this area; whilst Charles Abram wrote of a pebble bank on the shore behind the boulder clay knoll on which Banks Road had developed.[38] The use of such stones for building made these Crossens cottages unique in North Meols *(Fig. 8)*.

Fig. 7. Pair of thatched cottages.
These much-photographed cottages were at the junction of Dock Lane and Rufford Road

As in other parts of North Meols, the residents drew their water from shallow wells, which went about five feet down and had water standing in about half of their depth *(see front endpaper)*. The method employed was known as a 'pyggin'. A small tin drum was fastened on to a ladle seven feet long. The ladle was plunged into the well, and the water drawn off. (Interestingly, 'piggin' was an old Lancashire word for a small milk pail, usually wooden, with a long handle, which allowed it to be used as a ladle.) The wells were subject to contamination from surface drainage water, a danger exacerbated by the manner in which the dwellings and farm buildings were tightly huddled on Crossens' relatively small mound of high ground. A contemporary commentator observed that: 'The well and the privy lie side by side, in disgusting and dangerous neighbourhood. The filth of one flows directly, or by percolation, into the other.'[39] From the summer of 1795 small-pox raged for seven months in Churchtown, Crossens and Marshside and forty-one children died.[40]

There was a local absence of natural woodlands to provide fuel, although the growth of copses had been encouraged. Fortunately there was a local supply of an alternative fuel – 'torf' (peat). Access to peat turf from the Moss, for fires, was regulated by a bye-law of the Court Leet. The amount of peat that an individual might cut depended upon the size of his cottage

Fig. 8. A pebble wall. This Banks Road building still survives

or farm. Coney has pointed out that parts of the mosslands were set aside for peat extraction and tenants were '... allocated separate portions known as rooms'.[41] One observer, writing in 1807, described how: 'The peasants who we saw digging peat, or turf, had boards about a foot square fastened under their clogs to prevent them sinking into the bog.'[42]

From medieval times, the manor of North Meols had passed through the Coudray and Aughton families. Members of the Aughton family had been lords of the manor for some two hundred years when John Aughton died without issue in 1550. The manor then passed to his two married sisters and it was at this point that North Meols was again divided into two parts, or moieties, and the two husbands – John Bold and Barnaby Kitchen – became joint lords of the manor. The allocation of the land between the Bolds and the Kitchens was made in an unusual manner. Instead of a simple division of the estate into two large unified blocks, each family received a large number of smallholdings throughout the parish. Crossens, like other parts of North Meols, became a patchwork of Bold and Kitchen plots *(Fig. 9)*. A later marriage resulted in the Kitchen moiety passing into the Hesketh family. In the second half of the eighteenth century, the landowners – the Heskeths and the Bolds – granted leases for property in Crossens to members of the Abram, Ainscough, Barton, Boond (Bond), Brookfield, Copeland, Cropper, Gregson, Halsall, Jackson, Linaker, Ryding, and Wright families. There was one locally unfamiliar name, which appeared twice in the list of leaseholders – Jonathan Strange.[43]

Martin Mere, which skirted the eastern boundary of Crossens, was to exercise considerable influence on the village's development. The potential agricultural rewards for draining the Mere were huge. As early as 1692, Thomas Fleetwood of Bank Hall in Bretherton obtained a lease from the landowners and an Act of Parliament granting him powers to drain the district.[44] On the advice of Dutch engineers, he dug a sluice, one and a

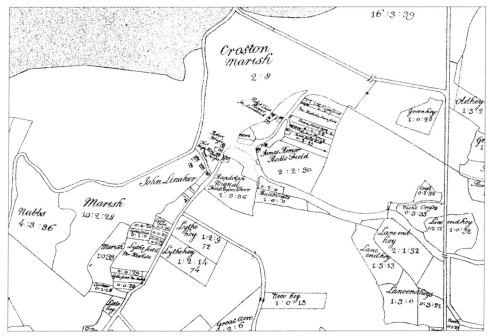

Fig. 9. An extract of Bankes' Map 1736. It shows the patchwork distribution of plots held in Crossens by the Bold family

half miles long and twenty-four feet wide, from the sea to the edge of the lake. It cut through the banked alluvium at Crossens. Something of the scale of this enterprise can be grasped from the claim that there were as many as 2,000 men employed in digging the new channel. Floodgates were installed which automatically closed when the sea rose higher than the water in the Sluice and opened again when the tide fell. Fleetwood also built a bridge, later known as the Old Sluice Bridge, close to Fiddler's Ferry *(see endpaper)*. Despite all these efforts and grandiose claims that he had converted the Mere into firm dry land, the scheme enjoyed only limited success *(Fig. 10)*. Periodic flooding still occurred, and the reclaimed land was little better than summer pasture. The lack of gradient across the beach meant that drifting sand quickly choked the floodgates, whilst high tides later washed them away. Almost 100 years later, Thomas Eccleston Scarisbrick of Scarisbrick Hall, whose estate included much of Martin Mere, recognised the potential benefits to be obtained by draining it. As he did not own the land where Fleetwood's Sluice met the Ribble estuary at Crossens, he had to obtain leases from the Heskeths before he could work on the floodgates. In fact he erected three sets of gates, including a pair of 'flushing gates'. During the dry season, when the flow from the

Fig. 10. Memorial to Thomas Fleetwood in St. Cuthbert's Church. The Latin inscription on this marble tablet records Fleetwood's achievement in draining the Mere

Mere was insufficient to scour the channel, tidal water was trapped between these gates and then used for that purpose. Although this system still depended upon gravity to get water off the Mere into the sea, it did bring a substantial amount of land into cultivation. In 1786, Eccleston Scarisbrick was presented with the Gold Medal of the Society for the Encouragement of Arts, Manufactures and Commerce to mark this achievement.

The Mere had long been a source of fish, and estate records contain many references to fishing. Coney has demonstrated that: 'From the landowners' point of view the most valuable asset of undrained Martin Mere was its store of fish.'[45] Fishing was a commercial enterprise, with the best catches, including pike, appearing to have been made at the inland end of the Mere. Nevertheless, fishing was also undertaken from the North Meols margin. In the fourteenth century, the lord of the manor of North Meols took legal action against two Rufford men for fishing in waters that he regarded as part of North Meols. A sixteenth-century document refers to 'Le Ele Fysshyng' (the eel fishery). Some examples of old Lancashire mossland eel-spears are preserved in Rufford Old Hall *(Fig. 11)*. In 1640, three men from the Scarisbrick district appeared before the Court Baron of North Meols accused of '… poullering in the wicke diche betwixt the meare and the hall of the Meales.'[46] They had been beating the water and spearing eels as they swam away. The fine of six shillings and eight pence (33p) was heavy and was apparently awarded in order to act as a deterrent to others. Later Bulpit wrote of delicious eels, locally called 'snigs', which were to be caught at the Sluice Bridge.[47] Clare, in his now scarce book – *A Short History of North Meols* – claimed that very large catches of eels were sometimes netted in Crossens brooks. He also reported that '… an eel trap in wicker-work was found in the … excavations at Meols Hall gate.'[48] Writing in the 1920s, Mr. Ratcliffe, of the Southport and District Angling Association, confirmed that for hundreds of years large quantities of eels had been caught at Crossens using traps baited with earthworms.[49]

Bulpit also uncovered evidence of North Meols men fishing on the Mere. One of his most cherished archaeological finds – a large dugout logboat – was found on a drained section of the Mere close to Crossens. A farmer, Peter Brookfield, who was one of his parishioners, raised it from a depth of about three feet in 1899. He thought that he was clearing an ancient tree trunk from the field, a

Fig. 11. An eel spearer. The local term for spearing was 'chopping'

common occurrence *(Fig. 12)*. Carbon dating has placed the boat as being from the sixth century, although a lead patch, which had been fixed with iron nails, and the presence of a musket suggest that it was still being used for fishing and wildfowling at a much later date. The boat was sixteen and a half feet long and four feet wide. It was the last and the only surviving example of the fifteen such boats which have been recovered from the Mere *(Fig. 13)*. These boats include one found in the grounds of Meols Hall in 1894. The leases granted by the landowners to the Martin Mere fishermen frequently included the rights to wildfowling. Some leaseholders also had the right to harvest reeds for thatching and to collect wildfowl eggs. Further evidence of wildfowling in North Meols came when two Roundhead soldiers entered the parish in 1642 seeking to commandeer firearms. Their finds were restricted to '… towe fowling peeces and towe burdinge peeces'.[50] It seems likely that many of the residents had been able to successfully conceal their guns from the searchers.

The first half of the eighteenth century saw the building of the Douglas Navigation to link the Wigan coalfield with the rapidly growing market for coal around the Irish Sea, particularly Liverpool. (This scheme pre-dated and was later superseded by the Leeds and Liverpool Canal.) The

Fig. 12. Bulpit and the logboat in Water Lane 1899

Fig. 13. The logboat in the Botanic Gardens Museum c. 1905

Fig. 14. The 'Fylde' at Hesketh Bank. This 'Mersey Flat' was used to transport bricks from Alty's brickworks

River Douglas was made navigable, with a series of locks, for boats carrying coal and stone from the Wigan district to the Ribble at Hesketh Bank. Sail-powered barges –'Mersey Flats' – were used for this trade *(Fig. 14)*. Interestingly, the engineer responsible for the Douglas scheme offered an alternative plan '... for taking the navigation from Rufford across Martin Mere to Crossens.' This would have shortened the distance to the sea by six miles and because of the tidal range at Crossens would have given better access for sea-going vessels.[51] His imaginative proposal was not adopted and one can only speculate on the impact such a project might have had on the development of Crossens.

References

1. Bulpit, W.T., *Notes on Southport and District* (1908), p.75.
2. Bailey, F.A., *A History of Southport* (1955), p.20.
3. Farrer, W., *A History of the Parish of North Meols* (1903), p.12.
4. *Southport Visiter (S.V.),* 2 April 1904. (n.b. the idiosyncratic spelling of *Visiter*).
5. Baines, E., *History of the County Palatine and Duchy of Lancaster* (1870 Ed.), Vol.II, p.433.
6. Ashton, W., *The Evolution of a Coastline* (1920), p.93.
7. Thompson Watkin, W., *Roman Lancashire* (1883), p.3.
8. Bulpit, W.T., p.89.
9. Bailey, F. A., p.20.
10. Bulpit, W.T., p.78.
11. Baines, E., p.133.
12. Wilkinson, J. (ed.), *The Letters of Thomas Langton Flax Merchant of Kirkham 1771-1781* (1994), p.125.
13. *Cheetham Papers, Envelope No.70.* Transcript of a diary of Mrs. Charles Hesketh.
14. *Lytham and St. Annes Express,* 26 July 1935.
15. Clare, R.L., *A Short History of North Meols* (1952), p.36.
16. *S.V.,* 16 November 1879.
17. All references to Martin Mere owe much to advice received from Dr. Audrey Coney.
18. Palatinate of Lancashire, Plea Roll No. 1 quoted by Aughton, P., *North Meols and Southport: A History* (1988), p.31.
19. Ashton, W., p.97.
20. Bagley, J.J., & Hodgkiss, A.G., *Lancashire: A History of the County Palatine in Early Maps* (1985), p.43.
21. Farrer, W., p.33.
22. Cotterall, J., *How Southport got its Churches* (1992), p.14.
23. *Wills and Inventories, Matthew French,* 1615.
24. *S.V.,* 30 June 1973.
25. Aughton, P., *North Meols and Southport: a History* (1988), p.24.
26. Bulpit, W.T., p.79.

27. Whittingham, T.E., *Around 450 not out* (1985), p.11.
28. Rideout, E.H., 'Poor Law Administration in North Meols in the Eighteenth Century' *T.H.S.L.C.*, (1929), vol.81, p.100.
29. Bulpit, W.T., p.78.
30. Raines, F.R., 'Notitia Cestriensis or Historic Notices of the Diocese of Chester by R.R. Francis Gastrell D.D.' *Chetham Society*, vol.XXI. vol. II part II., p.liii. (1850).
31. Farrer, W., p.33.
32. Clare, R.L., p.37.
33. Farrer, W., p.33.
34. Wright, G., *Southport 200 Years* (1992), p.21.
35. *An Insurance Claim Form for Peter Rymer 1749.*
36. *A farm lease granted by Robert Hesketh to Richard Wright 1754.*
37. *S.V.*, 18 January 1985.
38. *S.V.*, 27 February 1979.
39. *The Southport Daily News and Birkdale Chronicle*, 21 August 1874. (This newspaper, which gave coverage to the country districts around Southport as well as the town, regularly changed its title. It is shown as *S.N.* throughout.)
40. *S.V.*, 14 March 1935.
41. Coney, A., 'Fish, fowl and fen: landscape and economy on seventeenth-century Martin Mere' *Landscape History* Vol.14, 1992.
42. *S.N.*, 24 April 1875.
43. *North Meols Registers of Leases 1749-1801.* Transcribed by Cheetham, F.H.
44. Brodrick, H., 'Martin Mere and its Antiquities' in British Association, *Southport: A Handbook of the Town* (1903), p.199.
45. Coney, A. p.57.
46. Cheetham, F.H.,'The Records of the Court Baron of North Meols 1640 & 1643', *T.H.S.L.C.*, vol.34 (1932), p.17.
47. Bulpit, W.T., p.85.
48. Clare, R.L., p.38.
49. *S.V.*, 18 April 1925.
50. Aughton, P., p.67.
51. Clarke, M., *The Leeds and Liverpool Canal* (1990), p.48.

CHAPTER TWO

An Isolated Agricultural Village 1800-1875

*Every allowance must be made for the backward opinions of the villagers
[of Crossens] for hitherto they have lived according to the ideas
of the middle ages.*
Southport News and Birkdale Chronicle 17 October 1874

A T THE beginning of the nineteenth century Crossens was still commonly spelt as Crossons. This is how it appears in Glazebrook's *Guide to Southport* in 1826 and later in the first entries in St. John's Church registers. The change to Crossens appears to have taken place about 1840.[1]

The Residents

Unlike Southport, which experienced a dramatic growth in population during the nineteenth century, Crossens remained a rural backwater, a recommended country excursion for visitors to Southport. Thomas Tidmarsh, writing in 1842, advised a lover of rambling or solitude '... to wend his way ... towards Crossens, and he will find sufficient loneliness as well as loveliness of nature to delight.'[2] A guidebook published seven years later suggested that: 'The plain, quiet and rustic appearance of this village deserves a visit.'[3] One visitor, Miss Weeton, has left us an account of such an outing in her journal. Whilst staying in Southport in 1823, she hired a horse and rode along the beach to Crossens.[4] Another visitor, Mary Benson '... a serious minded Quakeress', recorded the events of a ten-day holiday in Southport in her diary for 1842. She visited the circulating library and consulted the published guides, but failed in her attempt to buy a map of the coast. Nevertheless, on a cold windy day in May she took an afternoon '... walk to Crossens and along the side of the sluice to find out Martin Mere.'[5]

Fig. 15. A pair of cottages with a slate roof and brick walls. This building was on the corner of Rufford Road and North Road. An old man called 'Blue Stick' lived in the cottage on the right. His name came from his custom of dancing round the village at election time waving a pair of morris dancing sticks. They were painted blue to demonstrate his political allegiance

The hamlet had grown up around the crowded Town Causeway (Banks Road), on the boulder clay mound to the north of The Plough. Poverty was widespread and at a vestry meeting, following an outbreak of fever in 1832, the Overseer was instructed '... to whitewash and ventilate the houses of the poor families, who are unable to bear the expense themselves.'[6] The residents were still dependent on the shallow, often polluted, wells for drinking water. Young James Johnson of Banks Road was paid a penny a week to carry drinking water from a well to the vicarage.[7]

From a population of 575 in 1851, the population of Crossens increased by just over a hundred in the following twenty years. This increase consisted largely of the families of poorly-paid labourers. Many of these workers walked to and from their places of employment in Southport in order to take advantage of the cheaper property that was available in Crossens. Bulpit observes that when he first knew Crossens, cottage rents were very low '... being £3 per annum, or 1s 6d (7.5p) per week.'[8] Despite the relative cheapness of property one Councillor, addressing the Southport Town Council in 1874, judged that such was the poverty in

Crossens that: 'Many of the cottagers were barely able to keep a roof over their heads.'[9]

Early in the nineteenth century there had been a little development back along Bankfield Lane (now Rufford Road) towards Churchtown. Date plaques on the front walls of a terrace of brick-built cottages, adjoining Land Lane, show that it was erected in the 1820s *(see front endpaper)*. Bricks came from neighbouring Banks, where they were made from the locally available boulder clay. Further small cheap brick houses were built in Land Houses. The walls of some of the old wattle and daub cottages were clad in brick, and the thatched roofs replaced with slates *(Fig. 15)*. As late as 1891 there were still twenty-two tiny one-bay cottages with only two rooms, and a further eighteen with three in Crossens. Behind The Plough and Rufford Road were the densely packed small terraced houses of 'The Fold', an unwholesome clutter of cheap property.

The 1851 census returns contain what were to become familiar family names in Crossens. The heads of household included thirteen Gregsons, eight Wareings and Blundells, five Brookfields, Linakers and Croppers, and four Howards, Wrights and Rymers (and a Rimmer). The instances of two or three families were Ainscough, Aughton, Ball, Baxendale, Chadwick, Gildert, Hesketh, Hosker, Johnson, Peet, Sutton, Tomlinson, and Watkinson. Out of the 104 households only ten per cent of the families had a surname which they alone carried. The fact that so many residents shared the same names led to the local dependence on nicknames, although Crossens families never rivalled the Wrights of Marshside in this respect.[10] By 1861 there were fifteen new family names; ten years later there were a further ten, four of which, however, were the rector, the village policeman and two schoolteachers.

The Landowners

In the nineteenth century a third family – the Scarisbricks of Scarisbrick Hall – became the major landowner in Southport, including Crossens. Charles Scarisbrick obtained much of North Meols through purchase. He had inherited the Scarisbrick estates on his father's death in 1833. His two older brothers had already died and, in a fiercely contested lawsuit, Charles was able to exclude his two older sisters and secure the title to all of his father's estates. Although starting from the disadvantage of being a younger son, Charles, a reclusive man of some mystery, had already amassed a considerable personal fortune in circumstances that attracted bizarre speculation. The fog and mystery which surrounded Charles Scarisbrick extended to his private life. It seems that he lived at Scarisbrick Hall with a former family servant, and between 1837 and 1841 the couple had three illegitimate children.[11] Scarisbrick knew that these natural children could not inherit the Scarisbrick family estates and that on his death these would revert to his sisters. It was to provide for his children that he bought into fast-developing Southport. As the children were excluded from inheriting any of the Scarisbrick estates, he believed that the Southport acquisition would continue to provide them with a source of income.

His initial negotiations were with the absentee lord of the manor – Sir Peter Hesketh Fleetwood. Hesketh Fleetwood was completely committed to developing Fleetwood and had little interest in North Meols. His ambitious scheme for Fleetwood was becoming a financial black hole that would eventually leave him penniless. Being aware of Hesketh Fleetwood's financial difficulties, Scarisbrick was quickly able to come to an agreement with him to purchase the North Meols estates. News of this agreement angered Peter's younger brother Charles, who had become rector of North Meols. He accused Peter of '... going behind his back' to make the sale.[12] Peter, not wanting to quarrel with his brother, went back on his agreement with Scarisbrick and sold his North Meols moiety (his holdings and half share in the lordship of the manor) to his younger brother in 1842. An experienced and successful entrepreneur, Scarisbrick was not deterred by this rebuff. Whilst negotiating with Hesketh Fleetwood, he had already approached North Meols' other lord of the manor, the financially stretched Sir Henry Bold-Hoghton. Bold-Hoghton readily agreed to sell his North Meols moiety to Scarisbrick. Scarisbrick did not have long to wait before he was also able to cherry-pick the prime parts of the Hesketh estate. As a result of his purchase of the North Meols estate from his brother, the Rev. Charles Hesketh had a large debt to service, and consequently he agreed to sell the major part of the estate to Scarisbrick in 1843. By this acquisition, Scarisbrick consolidated his hold on urban Southport, with its rich commercial potential. Hesketh retained his share of the lordship of the manor and some mainly agricultural land to the north of Southport, including the Hesketh Park and High Park areas, Marshside, Churchtown and Meols Hall. Scarisbrick, however, obtained Hesketh land in Crossens and Banks. This gave him control of the vital Martin Mere outlet into the Ribble estuary and the potential to further drain the area. Thus Charles Scarisbrick was joint lord of the manor and principal landowner in Crossens. By the time of his death in 1860, when his sister inherited Scarisbrick Hall and the entailed portion of the estate, all his North Meols purchases had been ring-fenced by establishing the Scarisbrick Estate Trust to administer the property, on behalf of his three natural children.

Under the provision of his will, 'The manorial rights and appurtenant estates' of North Meols were vested in the 'Scarisbrick Trust', which thus held the half share in the lordship of the manor. The stated purpose of the Trust was to provide the three beneficiaries with an annual income of £3,000 each, plus a further three-way division of any surplus funds. The original trustees included a surveyor and a solicitor, who were long-serving and trusted lieutenants of Charles Scarisbrick. They administered the Trust in a very effective manner. During the 1870s, the three children – William, Mary Ann, and Charles – never received less than £10,000 per annum each, with further substantial divisions of surpluses. Southport saw nothing of them during this period. They had been discreetly brought up in distant Germany. In a letter to one of the trustees in 1863, the twenty-six-year-old William declared that '… it is not my brother's or my intention to ever live in England.'[13]

Agriculture

In addition to the usual arable crops of wheat, barley, and potatoes, there were extensive tracts of meadow land at Crossens. Cattle grazed the summer pastures of Crossens Common Moss, which was well inland from the village, on the fringe of the Mere. Sheep were normally put out on the coastal marshes, though cattle were also grazed there. In the sixteenth century Camden had noted that 'magnificent black longhorns' were the dominant cattle in Lancashire.[14] Robert Seddon, a retired farmer whose family had farmed Old Midge Hall Farm for several generations, identified shorthorns as the locally favoured breed in the late nineteenth and early twentieth centuries. In 1874 there was a tragic accident when a young boy – Gregson – was killed tending cattle, whilst his father and mother were at market. One of his father's three cows strayed off the marsh, and he tried to return it by tying a rope to its horns and around his waist. The cow dragged him along Banks Road and he died from the injuries he received.[15] The Crossens farmers had formed a 'Cow Club' as a form of mutual insurance against their beasts suffering an accidental death. Such clubs were common in this area; the Southport club met at the Old Duke's Original Hotel. The Crossens Club met four times a year at The Plough. Details of the charges and payments are included in a rulebook, published in 1858 *(Fig. 16).*[16]

In order to enable horses to work on the damp low-lying lands fringing the Mere, the farmers placed large wooden plates, locally known as 'pattens', on their hooves. Two leather straps secured these plates. Two horses were frequently required to pull a plough through the heavy ground. Local moss

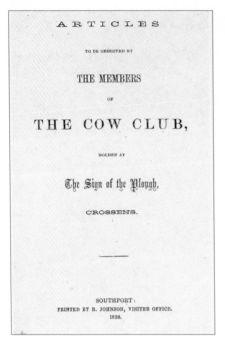

ARTICLES

TO BE OBSERVED BY

THE MEMBERS

OF

THE COW CLUB,

HOLDEN AT

The Sign of the Plough,

CROSSENS.

SOUTHPORT:
PRINTED BY R. JOHNSON, VISITER OFFICE.
1858.

Fig. 16. Articles of the Cow Club 1858

carts had unusually wide wheels to prevent them sinking into the soft ground *(See front jacket)*.

Almost every farm and cottage would have at least one pigsty in the yard, where there would also be chickens picking and scratching. Many of the cottagers kept their own breeding sow. When there was a pig to be killed the slaughter was usually done by a local butcher. 'Little Jack', an itinerant butcher from Banks, later undertook this task in much of North Meols. The pig had to be manhandled onto a four-legged trestle, where it was tied with its head hanging over the end *(Fig. 17)*. The snout was bound to prevent it from biting and squealing. Sticking it in the head with a spike, or bolt, killed it. 'Little Jack' had a spring-loaded gun for this task. After the pig's throat had been cut, a pail was placed to catch the blood, which had to be stirred to prevent coagulation. The blood was used in the making of black puddings, locally known as 'black jots'. After slaughter, the pig was scalded and the bristles scraped off before butchering. The meat was rubbed in salt, small amounts of saltpetre were also used in the curing process and ham was left in the salt longer than bacon. The fat was cut off the carcass and rolled up prior to 'rendering'. Rendering consisted of cutting up the fat, heating it in the oven until it became liquid, then bottling the lard for use in cooking. Some of the fat was cut into tiny cubes for inclusion in black puddings. My maternal great-grandmother regularly made black puddings and, as a small girl, my mother stood the market selling them.

As the new seaside town of Southport grew, it provided a market for local produce. In the 1840s there was an open-air market on Wednesdays and Saturdays, when '... farmers' carts hailing from Halsall, Scarisbrick, Crossens and Banks, brought vegetables, fruit, butter and eggs, and the owners spread out their baskets and hampers on the ground.'[17] Southport's first market was on Lords Street, as it was first called, opposite where the Prince of Wales Hotel now stands. As the small farmers sold their produce directly to the public, Saturday was their busiest day '...for they must attend market or see after huckstering (hawking).'[18] Making the journey to Preston market was

Fig. 17. A pig being slaughtered

more problematic; one commentator wrote of '... the poor horses dragging loads of produce over so-called roads in the Banks.'[19]

As the century progressed more land was brought under cultivation as new turf sea-banks enclosed the marsh. In order to protect these banks, a bye-law, of 1805, forbade residents from getting '... sand, slutch, or marl from within forty yards of any sea-cop.'[20] In 1809 Peter Hesketh Fleetwood, despite his preoccupation with developing Fleetwood, built a new sea-wall from Bank Nook in Marshside to Dock Lane near The Plough *(see front endpaper)*. Much of the work was undertaken by labourers from his Fleetwood estate, which led to it being dubbed 'Rossall Men's Bank'. Dickson in his 1815 *Views on the Agriculture of Lancashire* wrote that: 'Along the sea coast about North Mails [sic] ... there is a great deal of low sod or earth embankment.'[21] Periodically these banks were pierced by the tide and the farms suffered considerable damage. Dickson noted that the banks were '... uncommonly expensive in their repairs.' Invoices from the late 1870s suggest that a labourer be regularly employed 'repairing sea-bank'.[22] Breakwaters made from tree branches afforded the banks limited protection from wave action *(Fig. 18)*. The areas beyond the sea-cops were known as 'saltings', where the landowner encouraged the enlargement of the marsh by planting '... large numbers of sods'

25

Fig. 18. A labourer working on a sea-bank. The wooden palisade protected the bank from wave action

Fig. 20. Grass plantings on the saltings

Fig. 19. Hauling sods over the saltings on a sledge

(Fig. 19).[23] The marsh would then build up as the grass trapped mud from the Ribble *(Fig. 20).*

Crossens extended inland beyond the present municipal boundary, to the old North Meols parish boundary at the margin of Martin Mere. The precise boundary of this agricultural land was difficult to determine because of the periodic changes in the extent of the Mere. The farmers normally held their farms on leases of three lives. In 1851, there were twenty-two farms in Crossens occupying some 778 acres. Seven larger farms, between forty-eight and sixty-eight acres, accounted for half of this total; there were nine farms with between thirty and thirty-nine acres, and five small farms of under eleven acres. The extent to which farming dominated Crossens can be seen by the occupation of the heads of the hamlet's 104 inhabited houses. In addition to the twenty-two farmers there were thirty-three agricultural labourers; and many family members, including women, also worked on the land *(Fig. 21).* The women wore striped linsey skirts, protected by a brat (apron), and a large broad-brimmed bonnet was invariably worn. The local form of farming was labour-intensive; and as the farmers on these relatively small units worked in the fields alongside their workers, the social distance between them and the labourers was not as great as that found on much bigger farms in other parts of the country. Unlike the practice in Birkdale, the large majority of farm workers in Crossens were day labourers, living in their own cottages, rather than farm servants, living on the farm. They frequently cultivated their own plot of ground and kept a few pigs. These agricultural labourers fell into two distinct categories. There were the relatively more skilled teamsmen, who would tend and work a farm's horses, and who were employed on a permanent basis; whilst other labourers, who undertook routine tasks throughout the year, were still only semi-permanent, frequently working on piece rates. The increased demand for labour at harvest time brought children, hand-loom weavers and migrant Irish labourers into the fields *(Fig. 22).*

At the census of 1851, the hamlet had two smithies, those of James Brookfield and James Peet; whilst to make and repair carts, there was the wheelwright's shop of Richard Holmes. All three families were to continue to serve this agricultural community for many years. The enumerator's returns show John Baxendale, a corn dealer, who had Thomas Barron, a corn miller and his family living with him. Very unusually, in a hamlet where all the other householders involved in farming were born within the North Meols parish, both of these men came from Longton. Unfortunately, in identifying residents' places of birth, the census enumerator did not differentiate between the separate hamlets of North Meols. Clearly not all the householders were

Fig. 21. Reaping, raking and sheaf binding

Fig. 22. Potato picking

born in Crossens. For example, James Foster, the hamlet's only carter, was born in Moss Lane Churchtown, where his father John had a small seven-acre farm and was also a tailor. James was my great-grandfather and I vaguely recall being told that he had his own cart, a fact confirmed on my grandfather's birth certificate, and that he used to take farm produce to market. I have memories of being told of very early morning journeys to Liverpool market, following which James, tired but refreshed, slept on the return journey, whilst the horse both pulled and navigated the cart back to Crossens. Ten years later there were four carters in Crossens.

Agriculture continued to dominate life in Crossens. By 1861 the area farmed had grown to 976 acres, but the most significant change was the emergence of larger farms. Fourteen farms, of more than forty acres each, accounted for ninety per cent of the land under cultivation, leaving only 101 acres for the remaining five small farms. The number of farmers had fallen slightly to nineteen, but the number of heads of household who were agricultural labourers had grown to fifty-three. 'Charles Scarisbrick financed the construction of numerous farmhouses and outbuildings throughout his extensive estates between 1835 and 1843.' Always a schemer and seldom a philanthropist, this initiative appears to have been related to his legal ability to seek payment for the extensive drainage work that he was undertaking.[24]

There was one other major change in the Crossens agricultural scene. In 1813 the sea damaged the two outer gates of the triple set which Thomas Eccleston Scarisbrick of Scarisbrick Hall had built on The Sluice in 1783. His son Thomas replaced the gates with cast-iron cylinders equipped with valves, and the bridge, which carried the road to Banks, became known as Cylinder Bridge (see front endpaper). A stone gave its date as 1814. By 1853 Thomas's son, Charles Scarisbrick, held the Scarisbrick estate. He erected a steam-powered pumping station at Crossens to lift the water from the low-lying Sluice into Crossens Pool, at any state of the tide. The Crossens Pool Channel across the beach was also canalised. In such a flat landscape, the tall chimney of the pumping station proved to be a towering landmark. Associated drainage work included the diversion of the outlet of the New Pool, from Churchtown, under Bankfield Lane (now Rufford Road) by the side of Crossens church to the deep main drain. In order to increase the flow at Crossens, Scarisbrick diverted as many ditches as he could into the main drain. 'While the work was in progress a chaise, with two gentlemen riding in haste to Southport one night, was precipitated into the excavation and the horse was killed.'[25] A Churchtown resident recalled that the Mere farmers '... burned the moss and would get good crops without manure, by spreading the ashes on the land.'[26]

Fig. 23. The pumping station and mill

Charles Scarisbrick put a stop to this practice by threatening his tenants with eviction if they persisted. He claimed that such burning caused the level of the land to fall and thus increased the likelihood of flooding.

Scarisbrick also built a steam-powered corn mill, alongside the new pumping station, and it appears the same engineers cared for both facilities *(Fig. 23)*. The 1861 census returns show that new residents included William Chew, born in Ormskirk, who was a journeyman corn miller, and the Molyneux brothers – twenty-seven-year-old James and twenty-two-year-old Henry – both born in Wrightington, and recorded as 'engine drivers for the corn mill'. Joseph Leadbetter, the miller at Churchtown and later at Ainsdale, claimed that Charles Scarisbrick's agent had offered him the post of manager of the mill at Crossens, but he had turned it down when he was offered a partnership in the Hesketh's Churchtown mill.[27] By 1871, another journeyman miller and an apprentice, Chew's thirteen-year-old son, had joined him in Crossens mill. The mill was prospering because of the reliability of its steam power, compared with the erratic wind power on which other local mills depended.

By 1871 the area farmed in Crossens had grown to 1,213 acres. Sixteen farms of over forty acres each still amounted to almost ninety per cent of the land, whilst seven smaller farms included two of only four acres each.

30

Fig. 24. Horse waiting outside Moss Lane smithy

Four of the farmers were incomers from outside the parish. The number of agricultural labourers was almost the same as a decade earlier. Contemporary invoices shed some light on the condition of these labourers. Isaac Cotterall, the only agricultural labourer in Crossens who had been born outside the parish, was employed for twenty-five days in May 1878, 'Looking after cattle on Meols Mere', and the rate of pay was 3s 4d (17p) a day.[28] The number of blacksmiths remained very much as it was *(Fig. 24)*, but the wheelwright trade in Crossens appeared to have been cornered by John Tomlinson, the licensee of The Plough. He employed four men in his workshop. His printed billhead, from the 1870s, also described Tomlinson as an 'agent for agricultural implements and machinery of every description'. Like his predecessors at The Plough, Tomlinson was also a farmer and ran the adjoining 100-acre Plough Farm. In 1875, he gave a review of farming in Crossens to the *Southport Daily News and Birkdale Chronicle*:

> Mr. Tomlinson of Crossens, considers wheat as offering a rather inferior sample, and oats nothing to be compared with last year. Turnips are pretty fair, and mangolds going ahead. The second crop of hay beats the first both in quantity and quality. Potatoes are very bad, and the season has been too wet for carrots.

At a time when foot-and-mouth disease was raging along the south-west Lancashire coast, he went on to state that there had been '… no appearance of disease amongst the live-stock in Crossens.'[29]

Hand-loom Weaving

As in other poor agricultural villages to the north of Southport, farm labourers and their families, and even small-scale farmers, attempted to supplement their earnings by hand-loom weaving. Entries in the parish registers show that there were weavers in North Meols from the eighteenth century. There is evidence that flax was grown and worked locally: Bulpit writes of flax pits at Crossens, on the shore of North Meols Bay.[30] It appears, however, that cotton was more commonly woven, particularly for making canvas and sailcloth. Sailcloth was not only for boats, it was also used on windmill sails. Entries in Nicholas Blundell's *Great Diurnal* show that he regularly bought such fabric from North Meols.[31] In North Meols, the lords of the manor had forbidden the erection of any cotton mills and hand-loom weaving was a poorly remunerated cottage industry. The work came from agents from Chorley and Preston, locally known as 'putters out'. Sadly, the growing dependence of the poor North Meols families on the proceeds of their hand-looms coincided with the rapid mechanisation of the industry. Such was the severity of the distress faced by local hand-loom weavers, that they sent a petition to the Quarter Sessions in 1813. In 1826 George Greatbatch and William Alexander, local Independent ministers, raised a fund on their behalf. Faced by '… large demands made upon the funds of the parish for the payment of cottage rents, and the great increase of the improvident poor', a meeting of the parish vestry in 1831 decided '… to erect forthwith' a large workhouse '… with a requisite number of looms.'[32] It was to be on a ten-acre plot and arrangements were made to borrow £1,000 on the security of the parish poor rates. The scheme did not come to fruition, possibly foundering on the landowners' opposition to mills.

It seems that the mechanisation of the more specialist silk industry lagged behind the rapid pace of change experienced with cotton, and the local hand-loom weavers changed to silks and specialist light cottons. Bailey reports that Mr. Barton of Macclesfield, who had established a silk mill at Ormskirk, employed the North Meols silk weavers.[33] The 1851 census returns confirm that there was a change to silk in Crossens. There were nine heads of household and twenty-six others listed as weavers; many of these were members of weavers' or agricultural workers' families. Twenty-six of the thirty-five weavers worked with silk, the rest produced satin.

Writing of the local hand-loom weavers, Eric Glasgow noted that: 'John Baxendale of Crossens employed many of the weavers and kept the chief store in North Meols.[34] Could this be the John Baxendale who had been born in Longton, and is listed as a corn dealer and farmer in the census returns of 1851? Further industrial innovations, however, accelerated the pace of change and hand-loom weavers were doomed. By 1857 the *Southport Visiter* reported that only fifty of the 1,000 looms in the parish were working.[35] The American Civil War and the consequent loss of raw material led to further damage to the cotton industry. Most authorities say that this led to the demise of the weaving industry in North Meols. In 1861, however, there were still twenty-seven people in Crossens involved in weaving, of whom fourteen were householders. Fourteen were silk weavers; the number of satin weavers had dropped to two; surprisingly there were seven making cottons; whilst four weavers were recorded as 'mixed'. It is even more surprising to discover that ten years later, there were still six weavers in Crossens. One was seventy-four-year-old Nanny Watkinson. Her fifty-year-old son, who lived with her, was also a weaver. Only two male householders – Henry Watkinson and William Rimmer – were weavers. As Henry's wife was also a weaver, Watkinsons accounted for four of Crossens' six weavers. The returns supply no details as to what material these six wove. This was the last occasion when weavers appeared in the local census returns. Nevertheless, three years later, a Southport Town Councillor disparagingly referred to Churchtown and Crossens as '... a cotton and silk weaving place'.[36] Spindles and bobbins, used by local weavers can still be seen in the Botanic Gardens Museum.

The Village

In 1851 Crossens had a few basic traders. Ellen Blundell ran a grocer's shop with her two daughters and John Linaker was a grocer and draper. Both of these shops were still trading twenty years later, when they had been joined by a third shop run by William Leatherbarrow from Scarisbrick, who was also a stonemason. The Leatherbarrows had the largest house in Banks Road; it had three storeys, and their son was to become the long-serving master of the village school. The Plough was one of the oldest licensed houses in North Meols. Bulpit writes of there having been four inns in Crossens, including The Black Bull, at the corner where the 'Sloat', a steep narrow path, met Banks Road and another on the site of the Co-operative Store in Bankfield (Rufford) Lane. In 1851, however, Crossens' only innkeeper was twenty-seven-year-old John

Blundell, who kept The Plough. Interestingly, the articles of the Cow Club, published in 1858, refer to this inn as 'The Sign of the Plough' *(see Fig. 16)*. By 1861, fifty-three-year-old John Parkinson from Goosnargh was landlord. Ten years later John Tomlinson had succeeded him. All three were also farmers. There was one other beerseller in Crossens in 1851 – Richard Sutton, a nephew of 'Old Duke' Sutton, who also had a small six-acre farm and was a cordwainer. By 1861 he was still a beerseller, but also the assistant surveyor of highways. His widow Cicely, a woman described by Bland as being '... a local character of some celebrity', continued to run the beerhouse until her death, in her nineties, some thirty years later.[37] The beerhouse was then known as 'The Boot and Shoe', and stood alongside The Plough. Could its name have been a reference to the fact that Richard Sutton had been one of Crossens' numerous cordwainers (shoemakers)?

Sylvia Harrop pointed out what seemed to be an unusually high number of shoemakers in the rural community on Birkdale Common in 1851.[38] There appears to have been a similar picture in Crossens, where there were no fewer than three master cordwainers and nine journeymen. There were still six in the trade ten years later, and four householders making shoes in 1871, but thereafter the number dropped. Another, perhaps incongruous, feature of local agricultural communities was the number of tailors. The poor level of remuneration that they received probably explains their presence in the cheap property of Crossens. Although there was only one householder who was a tailor in 1851, by 1891 their number had grown to six.

Outside farming there were a few general labourers and virtually no skilled artisans living in Crossens. In 1851, there were four pavers, a pathman, and two very elderly stonebreakers. Perhaps their presence related to work on the causeways and low-lying field paths around Crossens; or perhaps out-of-town Crossens provided the cheapest accommodation for these, some of the lowest-paid workers. The only other worker in the building trade living in Crossens was a journeyman joiner, who lodged with an agricultural worker. In 1861, there were two paviors, two stonemasons and a plasterer's labourer living in the hamlet. An interesting new occupation for a resident of Crossens was 'brick moulder'. It was Henry Blundell, who no doubt worked in one of the nearby brickworks in Banks. This pattern of trade occupations persisted: the 1871 census shows three householders as stonemasons and four as stonemasons' labourers; there were two paviors and sawyers, and one bricklayer's labourer.

Another example of the socially marginal nature of Crossens was the presence, in 1851, of a cheap lodging house. Something of the standard of seventy-eight-year-old John Wright's establishment might be gleaned from the details of his lodgers. There were six female pedlars from Ireland and Scotland; the only man was a male bookkeeper. Ten years later, John still had his lodging house but there were no lodgers present on the night of the census. In 1871 there was still a single lodging house in the hamlet, and again the lodgers were Irish pedlars.

Gamekeepers, the Mere and Coursing

There was no hunt in south-west Lancashire; the terrain was either too rough, too damp or too intensively worked. Shooting was the major sporting pastime, and coursing enjoyed

Fig. 25. John Tomlinson, a Scarisbrick Estate gamekeeper

an enthusiastic following. Around Crossens, drainage ditches defined fields and hedgerows were rare. Nevertheless, coverts and copses were retained as cover for game, particularly pheasants. The landowners jealously guarded their rights to game. Charles Scarisbrick was firm in refusing his tenants the right to kill hares or rabbits feeding off their crops. One tenant was given notice to quit his farm in 1858 after he had been found running after a hare.[39] The Scarisbrick estate retained the right to shoot every kind of game on the estate. Joseph Leadbetter, the Churchtown miller who grew up in the village, recalls seeing Charles Scarisbrick '... on the Moss in his knee buckskin breeches shooting game.'[40] The local estates employed a number of gamekeepers to supervise the game, and in 1851 two were resident in Crossens. Both bore the same name – John Tomlinson – but as one was sixty-five and the other fifty-one it is unlikely that they were father and son (Fig. 25). As well as a gun, the gamekeepers frequently carried long poles to vault over the Mere's broad drainage ditches (Fig. 26). The Tomlinson family continued to be involved in gamekeeping into the twentieth century.

Fig. 26. Vaulting a drainage ditch

Fig. 27. A snipe catcher – another of Henry Tomlinson's magic lantern slides

Crossens cooking pots were still legally supplemented by hunting the birds which fed on the marshes. Wintering ducks and geese were shot, a popular activity known as 'fleeting'. Snipe were also plentiful on the salt marshes *(Fig. 27)*. Smaller birds were also sought: for example, 'pantling' for larks. Pantles were long lines from which hung, at intervals, 'gilders' – horsehair loops. This line was stretched between wooden pegs a few inches from the ground. Grain was scattered as bait along the line. In hard frosty weather the hungry larks took the bait, became entangled in the horsehair and finished up in a pie.[41] Larks were also hunted using nets – 'cymballing'. Two nets were used. These were hinged to the ground and strings led from the net to a concealed operator. Two decoy larks were staked to the ground near the net and when other larks were under the net the string was pulled. In his account of Crossens, Bulpit writes of 180 larks being caught in one morning.[42] A delicacy enjoyed by generations of local residents was samphire, sometimes known as 'sea asparagus'. This glaucous plant was very abundant on the marsh. Young fronds of this green fleshy plant, with its salty iodine flavour, were collected, pickled in vinegar and later sucked off the fibrous stem. Wild mushrooms also grew on the marsh. It was later claimed that the best came from the sea-bank behind Aughton's Farm, which was on Banks Road.[43]

Coursing flourished locally, and the two lords of the manor – Sir Peter Hesketh Fleetwood and Sir Henry Bold-Hoghton – were both involved. A newspaper report describing a meet appeared as early as 1833 in the Preston Pilot – '... the different runs were beautifully contested, the hares being strong and numerous.'[44] In 1838 the Lancashire Gold Cup, valued at 100 sovereigns, was held at Southport, and dogs were coursed at Birkdale, Halsall, Churchtown and Crossens.[45] During this six-day meet 177 hares were killed. A report of the South Lancashire Coursing Club meet in 1840 included an account of the 'Crossens Stakes'. An 1848 publication described the neighbourhood as '... the best coursing ground in the kingdom.'[46] Thirty years on, coursing meetings were still regularly held at Crossens. In 1875, the South Lancashire Champion Coursing Meeting, which included competition for The Great Scarisbrick Championship Cup, was held at Guinea Hall in Crossens, over land close to Crossens Common Moss and Martin Mere. The Southport News and Birkdale Chronicle wrote of the events bringing '... great benefits to the town', and how they were of '... immense value to the hotel keepers, cabmen and lodging-house keepers.'[47] Newspaper reports also tell of local men being fined for illegally coursing hares in the Crossens district.

Fishing

Despite being sandwiched between the fishing villages of Marshside and Banks, the people of the agricultural village of Crossens appear to have had little interest in the sea and its harvest. The evidence in the census returns confirms this view. In 1851 there were no fishermen recorded as living in Crossens. In 1861 a single nineteen-year-old boy was listed, and ten years later just John Aughton and his fifteen-year-old son. Surprisingly, there is also little evidence of Crossens women or girls working as cockle-gatherers, a practice which was very widespread in nearby Banks. There were three Crossens women identified as cockle-gatherers in the 1871 census returns, compared with almost fifty in Banks. Bulpit reported that since the mid-nineteenth century cockles had '... been a source of wealth for Banks, and many families have made a living by gathering and hawking them.'[48] It does seem that the inhabitants of Crossens had a bond with the land rather than the sea.

There also appears to have been a degree of antipathy between the residents of the agricultural village of Crossens and their immediate neighbours, in the fishing villages of Banks to the north and Marshside to the south. Writing much later, the vicar of Crossens, the Rev. Roy Baker, claimed that Crossens residents '… were protective of their own and jealous of intruders.' An elderly resident told him that towards the end of the nineteenth century '… one Crossens Casanova, smitten by a girl from Banks found out the hard way. He followed his heart down to Banks and was promptly stoned out of the village.'[49] A popular contemporary jingle proclaimed:

> Marshside, stinking fish,
> Banks is on't brew,
> Crossens is the fairest place
> That ere a man walked through.[50]

Church and School

The majority of the eighteenth-century rectors of North Meols chose not to live within the parish. The poorly recompensed curates who undertook most of the parish duties normally occupied the old rectory at Crossens. A contemporary plan shows that it was a small building with only two rooms on the ground floor and three bedrooms.[51] There was no garden, although later references suggest that there had been an orchard.[52] The rectory looked out onto the marsh and must have been a forbidding place, particularly in winter. Following the Clergy Act of 1803, however, it would have been necessary for the rector to live within the parish. Ten years earlier the living had been bought by John Ford, an Ormskirk physician, who installed his son Gilbert. Gilbert was a well-to-do sporting parson, who also held the living of Ormskirk and chose to live in the society of that busy market town. He had no wish to come to the backwater of North Meols and argued that the dilapidated rectory was '… entirely unfit for residence, through no neglect on his part.'[53] (Despite its apparently abject condition, it was judged to be suitable to be the home of his curate.) Ford claimed that although living in Ormskirk, he discharged a considerable part of his duties. The Bishop accepted his plea and he continued to live in Ormskirk. He did move to the new town of Southport in 1826, when funds were provided for a twelve-roomed late Georgian house in its own grounds off Roe Lane. The 500-year-old rectory at Crossens was demolished.

Despite the proximity of Crossens to the North Meols Parish Church of St. Cuthbert's, Bulpit claims that in the early nineteenth century Anglicans in Crossens worshipped in the old tithe barn, near to the Sluice. In 1835 the Rev. Charles Hesketh succeeded to the North Meols living and moved to the rectory in Roe Lane. Hesketh brought new energy and enthusiasm to his post. William Alexander, the respected local Independent minister, wrote to his son telling him of

... a new and surprising revolution, which had taken place in this parish. The new rector and his curate are doing just what they ought to do; they preach three or four times on the Sabbath, and in houses, schools and barns during the week. Being brother to the lord of the manor, of whom many farmers here hold their farms, his influence is very great. The church, I am told, is filled.[54]

Immediately after his arrival, the rector wrote to the National Society, an Anglican charity that allocated grants to provide schools, expressing his anxiety to establish an infant school at Crossens. He claimed that there were '... 96 children between the ages of 2 and 6 and these, of course, unable to reap advantages of the schools of Churchtown.'[55] He admitted that a building at Crossens would also serve as a meeting place for weekly lectures. To strengthen his case he emphasised that this was one of the poorest parts of the parish – 'our people consist chiefly of small farmers at rack rents and poor weavers.' The National Society responded with a grant of £30, in addition to helping to secure a Treasury building grant for £100. Such grants, to aid the construction of schools, had only been available from 1833. A small school – Crossens National School – was erected in 1836 (the foundation stone, now incorporated into the perimeter wall of the new school, gives the date as 1839). The small, simple one-room building was built sandwiched between The Plough and a farmyard *(Fig. 28)*.

Having initially built a school/meeting room at Crossens, a church quickly followed. St. John's, a chapel-of-ease to St. Cuthbert's, was opened in 1837. Holy Trinity church in Southport was being built at the same time and the plan, said to have been the work of the rector's wife, was used for both churches. Sadly both had later to be rebuilt. The Crossens church was built on a site in Bankfield Lane, rather detached from the hamlet. It was built of bricks made in Brick Kiln Lane (now Station Road), Banks. Local farmers carted them free of cost. The land for the '... burial ground, vicarage, and glebe' was conveyed by Peter Hesketh Fleetwood, Esq., of Rossall Hall, to the rector of North Meols (his brother), for 'ten shillings of lawful British money.'[56] Glebe was land that was provided for a parson to help support him by farming.

An early benefactor of the church was James Hardy Wrigley, J.P. of Southport, a wealthy retired cotton broker, who was a local magistrate and a deputy lieutenant of the county. He and his wife regularly worshipped at St. John's, travelling to Crossens in his coach. Mr. Wrigley was responsible for providing the church with many of its embellishments, including the

Fig. 28. Boys outside the old school. The building with the fretted barge boards was the school.

enlargement of his own pew in order to accommodate Mrs. Wrigley's crinoline. His interest in the village and the welfare of its inhabitants led to him being known as the 'Squire of Crossens'. He had lived at 'Sandowne', on the corner of Albert Road and Leicester Street from the time of its building in 1840. In 1859 pupils from the school were taken on an excursion to Southport and during the day they paraded outside his home, in recognition of his being a generous supporter of the school.[57] This country church, in a parish devoid of middle-class residents, attracted a succession of wealthy benefactors from outside the district.

Schooling was not yet compulsory, but the 1851 census enumerators' returns show some three quarters of Crossens children between the ages of four and eleven recorded as scholars. The poverty of the inhabitants of Crossens was, however, reflected in the sorry condition of the small school, which was no longer restricted to infants. Excerpts from the headmaster's Log Book, in which he was required to make daily entries, give a graphic account of conditions in the school. The schoolyard was unenclosed rough earth, flooded in winter and a dustbowl in summer. Pools came up to the schoolroom door; attempts were made to drain the yard, but they were never sufficiently serious or successful. As a result the children were frequently very dirty when they came into school. The school had no sewered drainage or running water. The single room had a stone floor; in winter it was '... scattered over with straw to keep warm the feet of the scholars.' Indeed the children were '... permitted to have a dance to keep warm their feet'[58], whilst in summer, '... the school being open to the slates draws down the heat and makes the room oppressively hot.'[59] There were small frequently broken windows, and an ill-fitting broken door. A stove was fitted in winter and children paid sixpence (2.5p) each 'coal money' for 'firing'. The stove was '... totally inadequate to warm the room.'[60] There was no fireguard and children were frequently burned, some seriously. After annual government inspection of schools was introduced in the early 1860s the inspector placed a limit on the number able to attend this small school. The securing of regular attendance proved an impossible task. Entries in the Log Book chronicle the absence of children labouring in the fields at intervals throughout the year. An Assistant Commissioner, reporting to the *Schools' Inquiry Commission* in 1868, described the education of the average boy on this '... sometimes moory, sometimes sandy plain that stretches along the coast from Preston to Liverpool.'

> He is kept away at time of hay harvest and corn harvest, and of potato picking which follows... if near the coast, he is sent out to gather shrimps and cockles, thus attending school only five or six months in the year.[61]

Discipline was harshly administered, but order proved difficult to obtain in the crowded schoolroom, '... whilst failure and inaccuracy instead of success characterises the performance of the scholars.'[62] Furthermore, the building, surrounded by middens and the yard of a public house, did not fulfil the government requirements. In 1872 the inspector noted that a promised extension had not been built and the number of pupils was restricted to ninety-four, which was barely adequate to serve the village. The school had a succession of short-stay head teachers. Perhaps the situation reached its nadir in 1875 when an assistant wrote: 'I have rarely taught children as backward and ill taught. The master lives in a public house and has been seen selling beer.'[63]

St. John's had become a parish in 1860 and a letter to the *Southport Visiter* in 1872 suggested that the church was also in a run down condition:

> I was pained to see an ugly looking building, which my companion called the parish church of Crossens. The building was never beautiful, nor does it belong to any particular style of architecture; it seems to be compounded of a third the style of a Scotch Kirk one sometimes sees in

a poor neighbourhood, and nearly two thirds of a Puritan meeting house. The church yard was untidy, and the only house in the parish apparently fit for a gentleman was the rectory, which presented a striking contrast to the ugly forlorn and neglected church.[64]

The vicar, the Rev. William Cornwell, was a popular figure in the parish. He was married at the church and was a regular visitor to his parishioners' homes. He was particularly remembered for the diligent manner in which he ministered to the sick and dying during a scourge of chicken-pox. St. John's was not an ample living and Cornwell took in boys as boarders to educate them, and he was the last vicar of Crossens to farm his own glebe.[65]

Rev. Thomas Henrey, who had exchanged another living with the vicar of Crossens in 1873, found the church in such

> … a state as to be a sturdy rebuke to the churchmen of the neighbourhood. It was not in a fit state to hold public services, it was neither wind nor weathertight, and consequently an air of damp and discomfort pervaded the structure.[66]

When it seemed that the situation could get no worse for this poor parish a severe gale, in 1874, caused serious structural damage to the church. The thirty-foot high turret tower became detached and '… fell through the roof in one mass.'[67] The vicar was able to obtain the support of other churches in the district and St. John's was refurbished. 'A new bell tower, with bells,' was erected and it was claimed that it could be '… seen at a considerable distance from the village.'[68] A handsome new porch gave further protection from the elements, and the church interior was re-decorated. Sadly another great storm in the following year stripped part of the roof bare.[69]

It was about 1850 that nonconformist evangelists began to visit Crossens. Some of the earliest visitors appear to have been members of the Wesleyan Reform Church, who held a service, to the south of the village proper, at Land Lane End (about the site on which the Co-operative Society store was later built). During the service there was a severe thunderstorm, and the missioners and their small congregation were invited to shelter and finish the service in the nearby cottage of Thomas Watkinson, a hand-loom weaver. Religious bigotry was a fact of life, and Watkinson was later informed that he had '… done wrong in entertaining such a set of heretics, who, if allowed, would bring dissension into the village.'[70] The family were warned that if they continued to entertain the missioners they would have to leave the village. Not easily deterred, Watkinson invited the missioners to return and hold weekly meetings.

Fig. 29. Primitive Methodist Chapel, Rufford Road.

The small cottage soon proved to be inadequate for the growing congregation, and they moved to a barn on a farm at the north end of the village. This initiative coincided with the national upheavals and schisms within Methodism, and it was under the banner of the United Methodist Free Churches that this 'cottage society' developed. The barn was fitted out as a chapel and served this congregation for twenty-eight years. A stable adjoining the old barn was converted into a cottage for the Watkinsons, who acted as chapel caretakers. The chapel had whitewashed walls, wooden forms without backs, and a box pulpit. Candles provided the only illumination and there was a coal stove in the middle of the room. A small choir, accompanied by flute, piccolo and a fiddle, led the singing. About 1870, paraffin lamps replaced the candles and a small second-hand harmonium was bought. No one in the congregation could play and the Watkinsons' son was dragooned into practising and then playing for the services.

Methodism had fractured into several strands, and in the country districts to the north of Southport, Primitive Methodism became strongly established. In neighbouring Banks and Marshside it enjoyed majority support. Some residents of Crossens, led by Robert Rymor, appear to have been meeting from about 1861, and a Primitive Methodist Chapel was opened in Crossens in 1866.[71] A modest building, it cost only £200 and was known as the

Providence Chapel *(Fig. 29)*. This chapel appears to have had links with Churchtown Independent Chapel, where Richard Watkinson was choirmaster for fifty years, and each week the harmonium was carried from Churchtown to Crossens for the service. Unlike Wesleyan Methodists, who attracted the middle classes and aspiring artisans and prospered in urban communities such as Southport, Primitive Methodists were particularly successful in reaching working-class people. Their ministers normally lacked higher education and much use was made of lay local preachers. They were inclined to '... preach very short and... hold a prayer meeting often.'[72] Methodism was growing nationally at this time and the Crossens chapels would have gained support from the strong congregations in Southport, Primitive Methodists at Church Street and United Free Methodists at Duke Street. It seems that Roman Catholicism had virtually no adherents amongst Crossens families.

Local Authority

As a part of the parish and township of North Meols, Crossens was under the jurisdiction of the parish vestry administered from Churchtown. From its beginning in the 1790s Southport grew rapidly, and its prosperous middle-class residents wanted to be free of the control of this farmer-dominated North Meols body. For them, it represented the past and the interests of the thinly populated agricultural areas. It was a body whose financial priorities lay with repairing roads to isolated farms, rather than providing for the inhabitants and visitors to Southport. As North Meols' principal ratepayers, the businessmen of Southport wanted a local authority that represented their urban interests. Energetic campaigning culminated in the Improvement Act of 1846, which released Southport from the control of the parish vestry, and placed it under the control of Improvement Commissioners. This left the North Meols Parochial Committee with responsibility solely for the rural rump of the parish.

North Meols was one of the few parishes in England which had taken advantage of the General Highways Act of 1835 and set up a Highways Board, which was in effect a committee of the parish vestry *(Fig. 30)*. It is interesting to note that in the 1830s the North Meols Parish Surveyor regularly received boatloads of stone at Crossens Pool for road building and repairs. The surveyor normally employed five men at 2s 6d (12p) a day to unload this cargo. Thirty years later the accounts show that regular shipments of boulder stones, from the northern bank of the Ribble, were still being unloaded at Cylinder Bridge. The residents must have wished

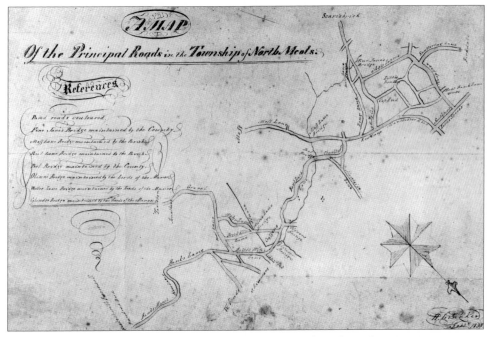

Fig. 30. The principal roads in the Township of North Meols 1835

that more of the stone had been used on the poorly maintained roads in Crossens. A 'Cross Un', in a letter to the *Southport Visiter* in 1875, wrote: 'Look at our Town Causeway and say whether relaying it is not needed. Look at the dangerous state of Water Lane by the railway bridge. How narrow it is and how likely for a conveyance to get into a ditch.'[73] Water Lane was notorious for becoming completely flooded and there was a permanent set of white posts to mark the track.

The parish vestry continued to administer the affairs of what proved to be a shrinking rural parish. In 1863 Birkdale gained administrative independence and established its own local board. Four years later Southport became a borough. In doing so it absorbed more North Meols land in the form of Blowick, Hesketh Park, Ecclesfield and Little Ireland, thus further shrinking the area for which the North Meols vestry was administratively responsible. Notwithstanding these acquisitions, Southport's predatory ambitions were not fully satisfied. By the mid-1870s it was targeting Churchtown. In an attempt to protect itself, Churchtown was considering following Birkdale's example and having its own local government board. Southport Town Council debated whether Crossens should also be included within the borough. There were strong voices of opposition, based on the primitive conditions prevailing there and the potential cost of improvements to the ratepayers of Southport. One councillor observed that these northern villages were '... not an area of building land'. Another described them as a place of '... dirty little lanes with no sanitation'. Many of the poor cottagers, he claimed, '... were barely able to keep a roof over their heads.'[74] The bottom line soon became obvious. As in so much of the municipal life in this area, it was the problem of sewage disposal that dominated. Southport, advised by an eminent civil engineer, was intending to develop a sewerage system that followed the natural fall of the land to the north and would discharge into the Ribble at Crossens Pool. Dr. Barron reminded his fellow Southport councillors that: 'If the Local Government Board was obtained in Churchtown, and if the Council attempted taking their sewer through there, it would be the cause of the greatest litigation that they had ever had in the district.' The incorporation of Crossens was vital to Southport as it needed an outlet for its sewerage scheme, and it wanted one which was well away from its central beach.

Crossens did not have a middle-class area similar to Birkdale Park, where the residents held and expressed strong views about amalgamation with Southport. In Crossens the vicar, one of the few middle-class residents, was a supporter of incorporation. There also appeared to be support from the members of the Methodist chapels. In the event there was no organised opposition to the scheme. The editor of the *Southport Daily News and Birkdale Chronicle* suggested in December 1875 that:

> If the good people of Crossens obtain only a half of the benefits which the Mayor promised them on Wednesday night, they will surely have cause to bless him when the village becomes part and parcel of the Borough of Southport.[75]

References

1. Walmsley, W.V., *St. John's Church, Crossens 1837-1937* (1937), p.10.
2. Bailey, F.A., *A History of Southport* (1955), p.85.
3. Sumner, J., *A Guide to Southport* (1849), p.18.
4. Hall, E., (ed.), *Miss Weeton: Journal of a Governess 1811-1825* (1939), p.232.
5. Bailey, F.A., p.87.
6. North Meols Parish, *Proceedings of the Vestry* (N.M.P.), 6 July 1832. (mss.)
7. *S.V.*, 19 September 1928.
8. Bulpit, W.T., *Notes on Southport and District* (1908), p.85.
9. *S.V.*, 19 May 1874.
10. Foster, Harry, *Don E Want Ony Srimps? The Story of the Fishermen of Southport and North Meols* (1998), p.113.

11. Liddle, J., 'Estate management and land reform politics: the Hesketh and Scarisbrick families and the making of Southport, 1824 to 1914', in Cannadine, D., *Patricians, power and politics in nineteenth-century towns* (1982). This academic study remains the most authoritative account of the influence of the major land-owning families on the growth of Southport.

12. Curtis, Bill, *The Golden Dream: The Biography of Sir Peter Hesketh Fleetwood, Bart., and the founding of the town of Fleetwood in Lancashire* (1995), p.88.

13. Liddle, J., p.151.

14. Camden, W., *Camden's Britannia 1697* (Facsimile edition 1971), p.787.

15. *S.N.,* 14 November 1874.

16. Anon., *Articles to be observed by the members of The Cow Club, Crossens* (1858).

17. Whitehead, J., *Recollections of Southport Fifty Years Ago* (1894), p.11.

18. *S.N.,* 11 March 1875.

19. Sumner, J., p.28.

20. Farrer, W., *A History of the Parish of North Meols* (1903), p.57.

21. Bailey, F.A., p.91.

22. Bray, D. L., 'Jobs and Jobbers in Mid-Victorian North Meols' in *North Meols Family History Society Journal,* Spring 1992, No. 3, p.10.

23. Greswell, R.K., 'Local Geology' in Bracewell, W.A. *(ed.,), Southport, N.A.H.T. Conference Souvenir* (1935), p.38.

24. Rogers, G., 'Lancashire Landowners and the Great Agricultural Depression.' *Northern History,* 1986, vol. XXII, p.256.

25. *S.V.,* 19 June 1981.

26. Garlick, A., (ed.), *A Miller's Journal by Joseph Leadbetter 1824-1905* (1999), p.204.

27. Garlick, A., p.240.

28. Bray, D.L., p.10.

29. *S.N.,* 6 September 1875.

30. Bulpit, W.T., p.82.

31. Bagley, J.J., (ed.), *The Great Diurnal of Nicholas Blundell of Little Crosby, Lancashire* Vol. Two 1712-1719 (1970), p.39.

32. *N.M.P.,* 20 April 1831.

33. Bailey, F.A., p. 27.

34. Glasgow, E., 'The hand-loom weavers of Marshside' in *S.V.,* 23 April 1974.

35. *S.V.,* 3 December 1857.

36. *S N.,* 19 May 1874.

37. *S.V.,* 31 January 1903.

38. Harrop, Sylvia, *Old Birkdale and Ainsdale: Life on the south-west Lancashire Coast 1600-1851* (1985), p. 126.

39. *S.V.,* 17 August 1898.

40. Garlick, A., p.204.

41. Hosker, A., *The Fishing Industry of North Meols* (1953), p. 28.

42. Bulpit,W.T., p. 87.

43. Howard, R.B., *The Aughtons of Aughton and North Meols* (1997), p.125.

44. *Preston Pilot,* 22 November 1833.

45. Bailey, F.A., p.165.

46. Robinson, F.W., *A Descriptive History of Southport* (1848), p.47.
47. *S.N.*, 6 March 1875.
48. Bulpit, W.T., p.48.
49. *S.V.*, 28 January 1978.
50. Baker, R.D., *Crossens: What's in a Name?* (n.d.).
51. *S.V.*, 3 December 1929.
52. Baker, R.D., p.8.
53. *S.V.*, 4 May 1935.
54. Bailey, F.A., p.112.
55. *N.S.L.F. Southport No.4. Crossens National File*. Letter 28 November 1835.
56. Walmsley, W.V., p.4.
57. *S.V.*, 26 May 1859.
58. *St. John's C.E. School Log Book*, 1 February 1865. (*L.B.*)
59. *L.B.*, 2 June 1865.
60. *L.B.*, 20 December 1869.
61. British Parliamentary Papers, *Report on the Schools' Inquiry Commission*, (1868), vol.IX, p. 703.
62. *L.B.*, H.M.I's Report 1872.
63. *L.B.*, 1875.
64. *S.V.*, 22 November 1872.
65. Walmsley, W.V., p.4.
66. *S.N.*, 19 December 1874.
67. Bland, E., *Annals of Southport and District* (1903), p.197.
68. *S.N.*, 16 February 1875.
69. *S.N.*, 28 September 1875.
70. James Watkinson, 'A Retrospect' in *Crossens United Methodist Free Church Lancashire May Fair and Grand Bazaar Handbook* (1904).
71. *S.V.*, 10 January 1925.
72. Rimmington, R.T., 'Methodism and Society in Leicester 1881-1914' in *The Local Historian*, May 2000, Vol. 30, No. 2. p. 79.
73. *S.V.*, 23 September 1875.
74. *S.V.*, 19 May 1874.
75. *S.N.*, 30 December 1875.

CHAPTER THREE

Incorporation and the Bulpit Years 1875-1904

The people of Crossens are all of the labouring class. They chiefly work for the Corporation or artificers and reside in Crossens because the rents are lower than in the town.

National Society Letter File

Incorporation

WHEN THE Southport Improvement Bill was presented to Parliament it included two objectives. The first was to secure '... the extension of the borough so as to include the two neighbouring villages called Churchtown and Crossens'; whilst the second was '... to raise a sum of money to enable the Corporation to carry out a system of sewerage.' This scheme, which it was estimated would cost between £50,000 and £100,000, was to have its '... outfall into a sort of rivulet, or river, into which the high tide came at high water, and in which there was always a supply of water.'[1] The rivulet was the Crossens Pool Channel, and Southport was to join Birkdale in using it as its sewer outlet. The seeds were being sown for a problem that would bedevil the district for years to come.

Churchtown and Crossens were duly incorporated into Southport in 1875, although the inland boundary was set at Fine Jane's Brook, thus excluding the scattered farms between this new boundary and the Mere, land which had long been part of North Meols parish. Similarly Banks, Crossens' northern neighbour, was not included in this extension of the borough. Although historically a part of North Meols parish, this detached rural village offered nothing that the Southport authority wanted, and was seen as a potential drain on municipal resources.

There was, however, much to be done if Southport's promises to Crossens were to be made good. One resident protested that: 'Southport was to take us under its wing, if we are under, we are covered up and forgotten.'[2] However, at a meeting held in the Primitive Methodist Chapel, Walter Smith, the Mayor of Southport and a railway contractor, promised residents of Crossens that in future there would be plenty of work for them. He recalled that this had not been '... the case five and twenty years ago, when he used to find working men from Crossens begging for a day's work.' He promised them two years of well-paid work '... near their doors.'[3] The West Lancashire Railway Company, which was to build its line through Crossens, would create the work, along with Southport Corporation, whose new sewerage system would involve deep labour-intensive excavations.

The West Lancashire Railway Company was formed to provide Southport with a rail link with Preston and East Lancashire. The Rev. W.T. Bulpit, then vicar of Banks, recognised its potential for the rural areas and enthusiastically supported it. Indeed, it appears that it was Bulpit who persuaded Edward Holden, the wealthy proprietor of the *Southport News*, a newspaper that covered the country districts as well as the town, to provide the necessary financial support for the Company. The first section of the line, between Hesketh Park and Hesketh Bank, was opened in 1878. Crossens station was on Bankfield Lane, on the southern boundary of the village. The station was built in brick and stone and because of the angle of the road bridge to the track, there were long driveway approaches to it *(see rear endpaper)*. The station was situated some distance from the main concentration of dwellings in Crossens, and special trains from Crossens to Southport were quickly withdrawn because of the lack of passengers. It was 1882 before the full line was open, giving Crossens farmers access to Preston market. Crossens station had goods sidings to facilitate this traffic, and there was also a large wagon shed for the use of the rolling stock on the line.

In addition to creating work during the construction phase, the railway also provided some permanent work and brought new residents to the village. The majority of the eight railway workers recorded in the 1881 census lived in New Lane. There were two platelayers, two platelayers' labourers, a signalman, a gatekeeper, a fireman, and the stationmaster. Five of these eight railwaymen had been born in North Meols, with two of them being from Crossens. These were a platelayer and a labourer, two of the most menial tasks. The stationmaster was twenty-three-year-old William Timperley, who had been born in Canada. By 1891 James Lunn, from Tarleton, had succeeded him, and was living in Brade Street. In 1901 the number of railway men had risen to thirteen, and of these eight were platelayers or labourers.

The sewerage scheme was delivered by 1878, but was to be dogged by troubles. It consisted of a main gravity sewer from Southport to Bank End at Crossens. There the system discharged into the Crossens Pool Channel; but the lack of flow and shallow fall to the Ribble led to a build-up of what a Medical Officer later described as '... solid sewage about five feet thick... from the Sluice Bridge to the mouth of the sewer.'[4] Every new sea-bank that was constructed lengthened the artificial channel that carried the waste waters to the sea. By 1886, the situation was so bad that the Scarisbrick Estate Trust was threatening the Corporation with litigation based on the 1875 Act, which made it responsible for clearing up the filth. Such was the stench, that residents in neighbouring Marshside and Banks derisively dubbed Crossens 'Little Muckington' and 'Muckington-on-Sluice'.[5] The Corporation faced further, possibly much more compelling, pressures from Southport residents objecting to the smells coming from town-centre grids. Because of the level nature of the terrain, getting the effluent through the sewers and away from Southport to Crossens was a problem. The lack of the necessary gradient resulted in very poor flow and a number of pumping stations had to be installed. The construction of sewers was hindered by the high local water table – the ream. Much of the subsoil consisted of waterlogged running sand. The scheme had already cost close to £130,000, more than a third more than the estimate and the Corporation went back to the Local Government Board for another loan of £13,000. At least the project meant more work for unskilled labourers. As the sewer was brought through Crossens the deep excavations reached down to a pebble bed and gravel from the trench was used to surface a path in St. John's churchyard.

Bulpit's Village and the Landowner

In developing Southport the landowners very deliberately pursued a policy of social segregation, exercising control through the covenants in their leases. The cheapest housing for the working classes was systematically relegated to the distant detached rural areas of Crossens and Birkdale Common. The poor, indigenous residents of Crossens were joined by some of the worst-paid workers from the town and other socially deprived individuals. Reports of meetings of the parish vestry contained many references to the social problems that existed in Crossens. The Medical Officer complained about what he described as the '... enormous death rate for children under the age of five.'[6] It seems that it was to Crossens that many unmarried mothers migrated with their babies. At a meeting in 1875, members of the North Meols Parochial Council were told of the plight of one servant girl, living in a room sixteen

Fig. 31. The Reverend William Bulpit with two of his daughters. Ada, on the right, was a teacher at St. John's school, her younger sister was Edith

by fourteen feet: 'She lives in a portion of a house... formerly a weaving shop. There are five of the family occupying two beds... There is only clay on the floor.'[7] Some residents further contributed to the village's poor reputation by regularly appearing in court on charges of drunkenness. Letters to the local newspapers demonstrated that respectable members of the Crossens community resented the village's poor image. One letter suggested that the residents of Crossens were '... cleaner in their persons and cleaner in their linen than the generality of the working classes in Southport.'[8]

Physical conditions in Crossens were also causing concern. The roads were in execrable condition. The vicar described them as being 'ankle deep in mud'.[9] Poor sanitation and the absence of reliable drinking water led to frequent epidemics. These problems were exacerbated by the high incidence of domestic pig keeping. Liquid manure from the swine cotes leached down into the well water. One correspondent in a local newspaper significantly suggested that although pig keeping might be permissible in Crossens, it '... should be taboo' and subject to penalties in Southport.[10] Farm middens added to the polluting fluids.

In 1878, the Rev. W.T. Bulpit transferred from Banks to become vicar of Crossens. He was a man of extraordinary energy and enterprise, an antiquarian and local historian who courted publicity and was tireless in raising funds for the parish. As a vicar he was paternal yet authoritarian, attentive to his sacred duties, but always aware of secular issues within the parish. Housing, drainage, a railway link, agriculture, schooling and adult literacy all attracted his attention *(Fig. 31)*. Crossens was without a resident doctor, and to fill this deficiency Bulpit also provided a form of medical service for his poor parishioners. He made herbal medicines, which he carried around the village under his billowing black cloak. Family tales tell of him also successfully attending to serious injuries and illnesses. Whilst at Banks, he had campaigned for the country districts to receive piped water. By 1875 the water company had laid pipes to Crossens, although not all the householders opted to take the 'town water', with its additional expense.

An account in the *Southport Visiter* in 1886 portrayed a very positive image of the progress that had been made:

> Improvements at Crossens are going at a rapid rate, and great credit is due to the Corporation for the liberal spirit in which they have considered the wants of the country district. The roads have now been paved with setts, and, instead of a rough jolting over boulders, carriages now gently roll over a level road... The dangerous

Fig. 32. Charles Scarisbrick – later Sir Charles, a generous benefactor of Crossens

carriageway has been widened, and jointly with the Scarisbrick Trustees, the Corporation are [sic] forming a village green with seats for pedestrians, from whence there will be a good view of the Ribble estuary. The work is now well accomplished, and an additional light has been erected at the new church.[11]

The three benefactors of the Scarisbrick Estate Trust had largely kept clear of the town. Nevertheless, the youngest son Charles and his German wife were persuaded to come and live in Southport in 1888. He was then forty-nine-years-old. His new home was Scarisbrick Lodge, at 41 Queens Road, on the corner with Leyland Road. Although his father was a Roman Catholic, the three children had been brought up as Protestants. Charles apparently formed a close bond with Bulpit, who had previously been a staunch supporter of his father. A stone tablet was built into the school wall commemorating the latter's life. It would seem that Bulpit orchestrated support for the Scarisbricks from their local tenants. In fact Charles adopted something of the role of lord of the manor, a title vested in the Trust, and he was referred to as 'squire' *(Fig. 32)*. As will be seen, it is with Crossens, possibly the poorest part of the estate, that the Scarisbricks were to enjoy a special relationship.

53

Fig. 33. A Rufford Road cottage opposite to Brook Street. It was the home of Tom Hosker, a tailor who for many years was the sub-postmaster of Crossens

By 1881 the population had grown to just over 1,000, and there were four grocers in the village. William Leatherbarrow, now also a farm bailiff, continued to run his shop, opposite to Rectory Farm; Ellen Blundell's daughters were still in business; and the newcomer in Crossens was the Co-operative Society, whose store, on the corner of Land Lane and Rufford Road, was managed by twenty-eight-year-old James Watkinson. The Co-operative Society had been introduced to North Meols in the 1860s, in the form of a store conducted in a room in a cottage in Churchgate, Churchtown, which had previously been used by a hand-loom weaver. In Crossens, the Co-operative Society also addressed the chronic shortage of sound cheap accommodation by building houses behind the store in Land Lane.[12] By 1891 there was also a butcher's shop, run by William Sockett, from Liverpool. In addition there was John Hesketh's bakery and the sub-Post Office run by Thomas Hosker, who was also a tailor *(Fig. 33)*. The 1901 census returns also show William Blundell, a herbalist, who brewed non-alcoholic botanical beverages, in Banks Road. Thomas Wareing sold fruit and greengrocery in Brade Street and William Bond had a grocery shop on the corner of Brade Street and Rufford Road. Next door, his twenty-one-year-old son Thomas, assisted by his younger brother Fred, was running the first of several

Fig. 34. Tomlinson's builder's yard from a window of The Plough. The pinnacles are those of the old schoolhouse. The Scarisbrick estate later used this yard. On the other side of the lane is Barton's Farm

cycle-making and repairing businesses that appeared in Crossens. There were several bakers, including Annie Rimmer of New Lane, who employed her son and another boy to make deliveries; Thomas Rimmer of Rufford Road, a master baker, and Sophia Mallett a twenty-eight-year-old spinster from Norwich, who the enumerator recorded as a 'cook, baker and confectioner' living in Land Lane. It seems that her business did not thrive – a 1902 directory describes her as a charwoman. Two boot and shoemakers (John Howard and Richard Wilson, who both had premises on Rufford Road), three tailors and several dressmakers also served the village. In addition, milk, egg and fish dealers were present, along with a coal retailer.

John Tomlinson continued to run The Plough, and in addition to the farm and the thriving wheelwright's shop, he had also built up a successful building business (*Fig. 34*). In 1881 he employed five joiners. By 1891, John's son Henry had succeeded him and in the following year he rebuilt the hotel. Significantly, the stained glass windows in the substantial new three-storey building contained the coat of arms of the Scarisbrick family. The Scarisbrick Trust agent used The Plough as his office for the collection of rents on local leases: one agent caused considerable local consternation when he absconded with all the money he had collected on a quarterly rent day. By 1901 Henry

Tomlinson was concentrating on his building business and lived in Rufford Road. Thomas Pye succeeded him as landlord of The Plough.

By 1881, the number of householders who were labourers had risen to fourteen. During the 1880s, further new houses were built in Brade Street, many of them were built by Richard Brade, a farmer who later lived at Sea View in Rufford Road. By 1891 seventy-four-year-old Gilbert Ball of no.6 New Lane was a road contractor, and the heads of household in Crossens included five road paviors *(Fig. 35)*. The number of other general labourers had risen to twenty-four, and there were a further four scavengers, but the number of skilled tradesmen only totalled ten *(Fig. 36)*. At the turn of the century the number of general labourers had increased to over fifty. Bulpit wrote of his parishioners: 'We have no artisans, labourers earn £1 per week with deductions for the loss of time for rain and frost ... people reside in the village for cheapness and walk to town for employment.'[13] Although this statement was not completely accurate, it certainly reflected the general nature of the village. In 1901, there were in fact fifteen artisans, or tradesmen living as heads of households in the village. In addition to these workers in building trades the villas in Southport created a demand for day gardeners. The first gardener from Crossens appeared in the 1871 returns. By 1881 there were four and in 1901 the total had reached nine. Notwithstanding the increase in the number of men following other occupations, agriculture continued to be the dominant occupation in Crossens.

Although the numbers of new names seen in the closing decades of the century grew, the old family names were still much in evidence. In 1891, the names Ainscough, Aughton, Ball, Baxendale, Blundell, Brookfield Chadwick, Cropper, Gildert, Gregson, Hesketh, Hosker, Howard, Johnson, Linaker, Peet, Rymer, Sutton, Tomlinson, Wareing, Watkinson and Wright still accounted for 127 of Crossens' 199 families. A similar pattern was still evident in 1901, with the number of Blundell, Brookfield, Gregson, Howard, Rimmer, and Wareing families being in double figures. At nineteen families, the Wareings were Crossens' largest 'tribe'.

In Bulpit, the parish certainly had a vicar committed to social improvement and he was able to enlist the active support of Charles Scarisbrick. During a bout of severe weather in 1887, the Scarisbrick family had undertaken local charity in what a newspaper commentator described as '... a quiet sort of way... without fuss or ostentatious display.' Money was '... distributed to families in Banks and Crossens who were for the time being unable to follow their calling.' Twenty dozen jumpers were also distributed and relief given to the sick.[14] In the 1890s, Scarisbrick levelled to the ground a number

Fig. 35. A road gang and steamroller in Crossens

Fig. 36. Scavenger and cart alongside Barton's Farm, Water Lane

Fig. 37. The small cramped terraced houses of 'The Fold'. The Fold was behind the Plough Hotel bowling green

Fig. 38. The rebuilt Plough Hotel and the houses which replaced 'The Fold'

Fig. 39. New modest, but solidly built, semi-detached houses in Rufford Road. They were nos. 204 to 210. Beyond the gap was the 1891 school extension with the Institute on the first floor

of '... insanitary houses' in the area known as 'The Fold', which was behind The Plough *(Fig. 37)*. The Boot and Shoe was lost and Crossens was left with only one licensed premises. In order to replace the demolished property Scarisbrick '... purchased a quantity of land from the estate and himself erected workmen's cottages, which were let at low rents.'[15] The 1894 Ordnance Survey map shows the first of these houses *(see front endpaper)*. The list of the first occupants demonstrate that they were mainly labourers bearing local names such as Blundell, Bond, Cropper, Gregson, Howard, Jackson, Johnson, Rimmer, and Wareing. Several of them were workers on the Scarisbrick estate *(Fig. 38)*. William Holder, who was Sir Charles' gardener and coachman for thirty-seven years, lived in one of the new houses. There are still houses on Rufford Road which bear the Scarisbrick coat of arms on their gables *(Fig. 39)*. One of the houses, no. 244, served as the estate office. The yard of Plough Farm, from which the Tomlinsons had developed their building business, became the estate yard. In all, Scarisbrick built nineteen cottages and five bungalows. He also built more expensive houses in this area. In 1896 a pair of semi-detached houses costing £415 was built close to the school *(Fig. 40)*. Henry Tomlinson, the former publican of The Plough who was now concentrating on his building business, occupied one of them

*Fig. 40. Building in Rufford Road –
nos. 200 & 202*

(no. 202); whilst a farmer -Edward Neale – lived in no. 200. In the following year this pair was joined by a very ornate detached house (no. 198), also built by Scarisbrick, which cost £307, and can still be seen alongside the school *(see Fig. 79)*. Thomas Baxendale, a retired farmer, initially occupied it. In 1897, the *Southport Visiter* claimed that: 'As many as 90 new houses have been erected this year, mostly on the high road from Southport to Preston.' *(see rear endpaper)*[16]

A few other detached houses, such as Mayfield – no. 235 – were later built on the opposite side of Rufford road *(Fig. 41)*. Crossens appeared to have been more of a village community than the other suburbs of Southport, since such lower middle-class housing as existed was not segregated from the poorer working-class dwellings. Two bungalows were built facing The Plough: one was known as Lady Scarisbrick's bungalow and was occupied by Miss Sarah Jump, Lady Scarisbrick's maid and travelling companion *(Fig. 42)*. Lady Scarisbrick's regard for Sarah was demonstrated when Sir Charles died and left her an annuity of £25 a year and a legacy of £500.

Church, School and Clubs

After arriving at Crossens, Bulpit immediately addressed the urgent need to improve the school, in order to retain its annual government grant. He decided to build afresh on an open site alongside the church in Rufford Road. He solicited 2,000 donations, mainly from Southport, towards the £1,000 required, and parishioners were persuaded to give their labour and services to help with the building. Dr. Peter Wood, a Mayor of Southport and a leading Wesleyan Methodist layman, laid the foundation stone.

Having obtained his new school, with accommodation for 144 children, Bulpit turned his attention to the church. He knew that he would again have to target his appeal for funds outside the parish. In 1882, a bazaar held at the

Fig. 41. 'Mayfield', no. 235 Rufford Road. A woman wearing a bonnet and brat, cleaning a window of this detached house

Fig. 42. The 'Scarisbrick bungalows' at the junction of Rufford Road and Banks Road. They were demolished to accommodate the roundabout

Fig. 43. St. John's Church without the tower – a rare photograph

Cambridge Hall on behalf of the new church raised £1,620. Significantly, all the churches in Southport had a stall at this event. Bulpit himself laid the foundation stone in the following year. Charles Scarisbrick, who had a pew in the church and occasionally attended services, was to become '… a generous benefactor'. The church, designed by J.W. Connon of Leeds, was re-built in distinctive yellow stone with red-stone dressing, at a total cost of £3,400.[17] The pulpit contains seven wooden panels, which were carved by a Susan Coalbank, an unusual achievement for a Victorian woman.[18] The church was opened before the building was completed *(Fig. 43)*. J.H. Burton, the Chairman of the Lancashire and Yorkshire Railway and a resident of Birkdale, later gave a donation for a 100-foot-tall spire, which would act as a landmark for fishermen. A spire was built, but problems with the construction meant that it had to be taken down and the tall tower replaced it. In 1887 the Scarisbrick family were the major subscribers towards providing a peal of six bells. Typically, Bulpit approached the Southport Town Council asking for a grant of £150 to illuminate the church clock to help shrimpers and sailors in the Ribble. He also wanted the clock to chime every quarter of an hour, which, he claimed, would help seafarers during foggy conditions *(See Fig. 48)*.[19] A master of such appeals, he cited the significant number of seafarers buried in the Crossens churchyard. The clock was installed and commissioned in 1889. It seems that Bulpit also persuaded the Corporation to supply gas to illuminate the clock free of charge. This concession was to continue until 1932. The tower was to prove to be very useful for William Leatherbarrow, the locally born headmaster of the school. In addition to his duties as schoolmaster, he ran a farm and the tower provided a vantage point from which he could keep an eye on his labourers during the school day *(Fig. 44)*. Bulpit also secured financial assistance from the Hesketh family towards the cost of building a new vicarage. The church prospered under the leadership of Bulpit, and harvest festival became an occasion for St. John's to show itself off and to

Fig. 44. William Leatherbarrow, headmaster of St. John's School

compete with the churches in neighbouring villages. In 1895 the harvest congregation, in the richly decorated St. John's, numbered over 700 *(Fig. 45)*.

Meanwhile, a further addition of an infant department was made to the school, for which Charles Scarisbrick's son – Thomas Talbot – laid the foundation stone *(Fig. 46)*. This extension increased the accommodation to over 400 children and the average attendance was about half of this number. Church schools in other working-class areas of Southport, such as High Park and Blowick, regularly experienced crises because of the shortage of places. Bulpit ensured that Crossens was never short of accommodation. Nevertheless, the level of government grant earned shows that academic standards at Crossens were not high. It is interesting to note that at one time an inspector reported that the school was overstaffed, a rare complaint in Southport. Bulpit complained that: 'I have overburdened myself with staff to improve the school and give it a fair chance.'[20]

Many of the children in this agricultural area finished as half-timers and then left school early. Describing his work on a farm, one former pupil, of nearby Churchtown Parochial School, later recalled: 'At about ten-years-of-age I was required to crawl on hand and knees pulling weeds after the horse-drawn scarifier.' His knees were protected by sacking tied around his legs, but

Fig. 45. St. John's – Harvest Festival decorations c.1895

Fig. 46. Guests at a church function. The group includes Charles Scarisbrick, rear row 2nd left, Thomas Scarisbrick, 4th right, and Rev. Bulpit extreme right. This occasion might have been the laying of the foundation stone for the school extension by Thomas. Note the local women seated behind the group, wearing their traditional dress

Fig. 47. Boys ducking in a trough at Plough Farm

he complained bitterly of 'back worche' (ache).[21] Although the school's Log Books regularly contained complaints about children being absent to work in the fields, the major cause of absence from school in the late nineteenth century was sickness *(Fig. 47)*. It is interesting to note that at a time when social provision and welfare were rare in schools, there was evidence that this dimension was recognised at Crossens. In times of depression a soup kitchen was opened in the school; Charles Scarisbrick gave a woollen pullover to every child; whilst a most unusual feature was the regular medical inspections and treatment of the children by Dr. Barry. He even performed minor operations in the school.[22] In August 1897 he removed two large growths from Ellen Gregson's tonsils, and a further two in September. Bulpit had not lost his touch in making appeals to the National Society for funds. In all he was successful on seven occasions. Perhaps he was guilty of a little exaggeration when he claimed that his '... district was one of the poorest in Lancashire';[23] but he certainly had a case in 1899 when he obtained assistance to repair the twenty-year-old '... board and joist floor' – Lancashire clogs had worn it through![24]

Between 1899 and 1901 a new feature appeared in the grounds of St. John's Church – the Scarisbrick mausoleum. Charles Scarisbrick had proposed its erection at a St. John's vestry meeting in 1898. There were no objections and,

65

Fig. 48. The Scarisbrick mausoleum dominated the churchyard

after consultation with the Consistory Court, permission was granted. The gritstone building was the only example of Romanesque architecture in Southport *(Fig. 48)*. Mausoleums were fashionable at this time, when there was distaste for burial, and a fear of being buried alive. The first of the twelve Scarisbricks to be placed in the mausoleum was committed in 1908. An unusual, but with the Scarisbricks, perhaps not unexpected, feature of the mausoleum is the complete absence of external inscriptions. It is impressive, but anonymous.

By 1879, the United Methodist congregation decided to replace their old barn chapel. The only site available was opposite to where the original cottage meetings had been held. Freehold was obtained, and to reduce the building costs local farmers did all the carting. The chapel was opened in 1880, and by 1904 the congregation had completely paid off the £2,200, which it had cost. In 1891 a generous gift of £1,000, from a Birkdale Park resident, paid for a new Sunday School building *(Fig. 49)*. Bulpit identified Miles Wright, Thomas Wright and James Watkinson as pillars of the United Methodist Church in Crossens. The Primitive Methodists also continued to flourish in Crossens and Robert Wareing was one of the principal members of the congregation. Bulpit said that the residents of Crossens were '… religious people, and total abstinence has taken firm root amongst them.'[25] This

Fig. 49. The United Methodist Chapel and school room

Fig. 50. A village funeral passes down Rufford Road. The mourners knew their place

Fig. 51. A procession to mark Queen Victoria's Diamond Jubilee 1897

statement might well have been true of the congregations of the two Methodist chapels, but certainly did not apply to all the residents of Crossens, as court records testified. The offenders included my great-grandfather.

Extensions to St. John's School, built in 1891, also included an institute and newsroom for the village. It seems that Bulpit understood the concept of a community school long before they became fashionable. In addition to the church, there appears to have been a fairly active sense of community in Crossens. There was a thriving 'Crossens Club'. Bulpit writes of William Gildart, a tall lusty man, walking in the front of the Club procession waving '... the big flag as freely as if it had been a toy one.'[26] The Club Day in June was a highlight of the village year. Such clubs provided members with insurance against hard times. Crossens Burial Club had an annual income of about £40 in 1886 *(Fig. 50)*. Bulpit also recalled two ancient local funeral practices: the giving away of 'funeral loaves', and 'the beautiful custom' of singing at the 'lifting' of a coffin. The village had another curious custom, which was to lead to one boy – John Riding – appearing in court. It appears that on the occasion of a wedding, a rope was put across the road to intercept the wedding party. On this occasion the horse pulling the cab was entangled; the fence to which the rope was attached was pulled down; and the boy was charged with the damage. The magistrates appreciated the nature of the custom and the boy only had to pay the costs.[27] Special occasions, such as Queen Victoria's Jubilee, were marked by village celebrations which invariably included a grand procession of decorated farm carts *(Fig. 51)*. Freemasons were active in Crossens, meeting at The Plough. It appears that Bulpit was an enthusiastic adherent.

Agriculture

The large farms continued to grow bigger during the last quarter of the century, and by 1881 Thomas Ainscough was farming 142 acres. Even this was not a big farm; and although it cost more to provide buildings on small farms, the Scarisbrick Trustees remained committed to them, recognising that they paid

> ... a third more rent than large ones ... The smaller the farms in this neighbourhood the greater the demand for them and the higher the rents ... Besides this class of farm is more easily worked by a family independently of paid labour, and are kept in a higher condition than large holdings.[28]

The 1901 census returns show that there were nineteen farms in Crossens. Rent was paid twice a year, on the first days of June and December. There was no rent on the farmhouse, only on the land. The estate maintained the fabric of the farmhouse and buildings and employed a number of tradesmen who undertook this work.

In common with farmers in other parts of Lancashire, the farmers of Crossens had been hit by the depressed condition of agriculture. The Scarisbrick Estate agent wrote: 'Ever since 1880 produce of all kinds has kept very low in price especially corn and potatoes on which this Estate is so dependent.'[29] Charles Scarisbrick and the Scarisbrick Trustees undertook further work on the Mere in 1882. The scheme cost £86,000 and included the installation of three very powerful centrifugal steam pumps *(Fig. 52)*. The steam engine for the estate's pumping station and mill was adapted to run on gas, which could be either town gas or gas manufactured on the site. In addition, gangs of men were employed to dig new drainage ditches. This work resulted in flooded fields becoming rarer. 'Martin Mere is now a scene of luxuriant fertility', wrote one commentator in 1887. 'Finer oats, clover, beans and turnips than those raised on this ground cannot be found anywhere.' He compared this improved condition with what he described as the '... rushy pastures of neighbouring estates'. He further claimed that there had been an excellent corn crop and the straw had already been sold *(Figs. 53 & 54)*.[30] A by-product of the drainage work was the creation of 'The Lump' – a large mound of excavated material alongside The Sluice. The greyish-blue clay from 'The Lump' (Blue Billy) was used to 'scotch', or line other drainage channels and gutters. Charles Scarisbrick also built another new sea-bank in the 1890s, which brought a further 1,000 acres under cultivation. This well-formed bank culminates at Crossens on the seaward side of the 'Bank End' sewerage works *(see rear endpaper)*.

The 1901 census shows that there were still some sixty agricultural labourers working on the farms, who were mostly born locally. A third of

Fig. 52. Water from the Mere being pumped into Crossens Pool

Fig. 53. Reaping by machine

Fig. 54. Loading a four-wheeled wagon. Plates have been added to enable it to carry a larger load

Fig. 55. J. Ball's outfit. A threshing machine, with a baler attached, both hauled by a steam traction engine, which also powered them

Fig. 56. A steam engine driving a threshing machine

Fig. 57. Scarisbrick gamekeepers. William Mayor, the head gamekeeper, supervises Bill Langden (later head keeper), Dick Palmer and Dick Tomlinson putting ferrets into rabbit holes in a wooded covert. The ferrets were muzzled

them were heads of their own households; almost a third were relatives of the farmers and lived on the farms; only two were non-family members in residence. Thus, unlike the pattern in Birkdale, the vast majority of agricultural workers in Crossens continued to be day labourers. For the first time the returns discriminated between teamsters, who worked a farm's horses, and ordinary agricultural labourers. The horsemen comprised approximately a quarter of the total number. Horses were sufficiently important to encourage a saddler to set up business in the village; whilst James Brookfield's New Lane smithy was now being run by his son Moses, who paid £23 to have a new smithy built in 1897. Many of the farms bred and raised their own horses. The larger ones kept their own stallion; whilst others chose to hire a sire for their foals on the basis of the postcard photographs, showing '… gigantic shire stallions' and quoting terms and conditions, that the breeders sent to them.[31] The 1891 returns showed a new agricultural occupation: twenty-five-year-old Henry Johnson from Banks was recorded as a threshing machine driver. John Ball, of Barton's Farm on Water Lane, became a threshing contractor, and his great Leviathan-like machines were a feature of the Crossens scene at harvest time *(Figs. 55 & 56)*.

72

Fig. 58. Netting rabbits in a ditch bank on the Mere

Fig. 59. Southport Royal Caledonian Curling Club c.1895. Members eating hot pot behind the hut

Fig. 60. Curling on a frozen field alongside Water Lane

By 1891, Charles Scarisbrick had installed William Mayor at the Shooting Box on the Mere, as his head keeper and watcher. Much of the keepers' work involved culling rabbits. Happily, a series of nine photographs of his team at work has survived *(Figs. 57 & 58)*. The gamekeepers were also responsible for organising sport for the landowner. Shooting parties were regularly entertained at the Shooting Box, where pheasants were raised. The wives on neighbouring farms provided 'setting hens' to hatch pheasant eggs. Robert Seddon, a retired farmer, described how Mayor, his grandfather, had to walk from the Shooting Box to Scarisbrick Lodge, alongside Hesketh Park, to give his weekly report to 'the squire'. It is interesting to note that Isaac Cotterall, an agricultural labourer mentioned in Chapter Two, had also become a gamekeeper. In 1901, two of Mayor's keepers, Richard Tomlinson and William Langden, lived in Moss Lane, whilst Richard Eastham lived in New Lane.

In addition to coursing and shooting, the area had become the venue for another fashionable winter sport for some of Southport's wealthy residents. Bulpit tells us that Water Lane, which led from the Plough towards Banks, was frequently under water.[32] When the large shallow pool froze over in hard winters, it was used for skating, and the Southport Royal Caledonian Curling Club rented a portion of it. The membership of this Club included several of the town's most prominent citizens *(Figs. 59 & 60)*. It had formerly had the use of Southport's magnificent glacarium and had been extremely active. The closure of the glacarium had left the Club with only this seasonal outdoor rink. The site was quite close to Banks station and the trains could be used for travel to Southport.

Fishing and Boat-Building

There were no Crossens fishermen recorded in the 1881 census returns. It seems that Bulpit might have been trying to exploit the romantic image of the toilers to the sea, when he sought outside support for a church building fund because '... so many of the Crossens people are poor

Fig. 61. Shrimp 'putters'. These hand-net fishermen, walking along the sea-bank at Crossens, might have come from Banks

labourers, cockle-gatherers and fishermen.'[33] Although fishing did not figure as an occupation of local residents, in the next two decennial census returns, it is possible that some could have dabbled with fishing. A minimum of equipment would have allowed a man to shrimp on foot, with a hand net – 'putting' *(Fig. 61)*. In the same period, no Crossens cockle-gatherers are identified, although there could have been occasional gatherers. By way of contrast, many men and women from Banks are specifically identified as fishermen or cockle-gatherers. Much of their cockling was done using carts to carry the bags of cockles off the beach. Some Banks cocklers used smacks, moored in the Crossens Pool, to travel to more distant beds on the northern bank of the Ribble. In 1901, three Banks fishermen were drowned in the Crossens Pool, when landing their catch in a heavy sea. They were transferring six bags of cockles from a sea-going smack to a small punt, when it filled with water and sank.[34] An entry in the school Log Book suggests that Crossens girls might have been employed by Marshside shrimp merchants to pick the shells off shrimps. In 1894 a lady Inspector of Factories, who was making enquiries about shrimp picking in Marshside, visited Crossens school.[35] The weight of evidence does not appear to support those modern local historians who claim that Crossens

Fig. 62. Boatyard at Crossens Pool c.1900. Because the channel was so narrow boats had to be launched sideways. The shed was destroyed by fire in 1901

had a sea-fishing industry. Bulpit appears to have got it right when, shorn of the need to 'spin', he asserted that Crossens residents '... disdained the shore, and would not gather cockles nor go shrimping.'[36]

The fishing industry was thriving at nearby Marshside and was supported by boat-builders and sailmakers.[37] The major shipbuilder was Peter's Dick Wright at 67 Shellfield Road. At one time, this yard was within 150 yards of the high water mark and Shellfield Road gave access to the Ribble estuary, close to Crossens in the north. Later, as the sea retreated, boats were hauled on a heavy-wheeled launching carriage, from Wright's land-locked yard to the sea front at Southport. Wright and Robert Latham, another Marshside resident, both decided to build and repair boats at Crossens, where they could get direct access to the sea, on the Crossens Pool Channel. Their yards were on the triangle of land outside the Sluice gates at Crossens. Latham built several large boat sheds there. The boat-yard's local name – 'Quay Nook' – was derived from a short stone quay, which was built on the bank of the Pool *(see Fig. 77)*. The channel was so narrow that boats had to be launched sideways. Contemporary photographs show a thriving small industry *(Fig. 62)*. There is, however, little evidence of Crossens men working in the yards. The 1901 census returns do show one boat-builder living in Crossens. He was Robert Rawstorne, who was born on the northern bank of the Ribble at Freckleton. As the tide retreated from Southport and the fishing fleet shrank, the building and repairing of the large yachts that the members of the West Lancashire and Corinthian Yacht Clubs sailed from the pier became a larger part of the business. In 1901 there was a disastrous fire at Latham's yard. It destroyed the boat-building sheds, workshop machinery, tools, timber and other raw materials, and most importantly eight boats. Insurance covered only fifty per cent of the losses. Nevertheless, both Wright and Latham were able to successfully transfer their businesses to Hesketh Bank, where the River Douglas provided a more reliable waterway. Rawstorne did not follow them to Hesketh Bank; he remained at 131 Rufford Road working as a milliner and draper. The boat-building industry had been short-lived in Crossens and the evidence suggests that it had little impact on the village.

Despite the increase in the number of residents who were finding work outside the village, Crossens entered the twentieth century as a predominantly agricultural community. Excursions from Southport to this rural village were still very popular. Wagonettes and landaus waited along The Promenade, with boards advertising 'Lovely country drive to Crossens and Banks, one shilling.'[38] This rural community was, however, soon to experience dramatic change.

References

1. *S.N.*, 20 April 1875.
2. *S.N.*, 23 September 1875.
3. *S.N.*, 30 December 1875.
4. *S.N.*, 15 July 1885.
5. Baker, R.D., *Crossens: What's in a Name*, (n.d.), p.2.
6. *S.N.*, 17 October 1874.
7. *S.N.*, 1 January 1875.
8. *S.N.*, 14 January 1875.
9. *S.N.*, 1 July 1875.
10. *S.N.*, 19 January 1875.
11. *S.V.*, 9 October 1886.
12. Bulpit, W.T., *Notes on Southport and District* (1908), p.78.
13. *N.S.L.F.*, no date.
14. *S.N.*, 2 March 1887.
15. *S.V.*, 28 January 1904.
16. *S.V.*, 24 December 1897.
17. Pevsner, N., *The Buildings of England: North Lancashire* (1969), p.236.

18. *S.V.*, 11 August 1979.
19. Cotterall, J., *How Southport Got its Churches* (1992), p.27.
20. *N.S.L.F.*, 24 April 1883.
21. Lloyd, R., *No Rehearsals, No Regrets* (1965), ch.5. p.5.
22. *Crossens C.E. School Log Book*. See 25 August 1895 and 15 August 1896.
23. *N.S.L.F.*, 15 May 1890.
24. *N.S.L.F.*, 28 August 1899.
25. Bulpit, W.T., p.86.
26. Bulpit, W.T., p.85.
27. *S.N.*, 24 April 1886.
28. Mutch, A., *Rural Life in S.W. Lancashire 1840-1914* (1988), p.18.
29. Mutch, A., p.49.
30. *S.N.*, 1 September 1887.
31. Lloyd, R., ch.2. p.6.
32. Bulpit, W.T., p.85.
33. *S.V.*, 23 March 1883.
34. *Ormskirk Advertiser*, 12 September 1901.
35. *L.B.*, 16 August 1894.
36. Bulpit, W.J., p.85.
37. Foster, Harry, *Don E Want Ony Srimps? The Story of the Fishermen of Southport and North Meols* (1998), pp.122-128. & Lloyd, L., *Southport and North Meols Fishermen and Boat Builders* (1998), pp. 39-50.
38. S.V., 16 February 1976.

CHAPTER FOUR

The Vulcan Fires Crossens 1904-1945

If the Vulcan Company had succeeded, people wouldn't have spoken about Crossens, near Southport. They would have said Southport near Crossens.
                                                        A former Vulcan worker 1964

Railway

ALTHOUGH THE West Lancashire Railway had successfully linked the farming and fishing communities along the southern coast of the Ribble estuary to the market in Preston, the new railway, unlike the Manchester and Liverpool lines from Southport, did not attract many first-class commuter passengers. Poor financial returns meant that the Company was soon in the bankruptcy court. Following lengthy negotiations, the Lancashire and Yorkshire Company took the venture over in 1897. This change brought an unexpected bonus for Crossens. The Lancashire and Yorkshire Company was pioneering schemes to electrify routes serving affluent suburbs. Its Southport to Liverpool line was the first steam railway in the world to be changed entirely to electric traction. This scheme was extended north beyond Southport, on the former West Lancashire line, to serve the developing high-class residential area of Hesketh Park, and was continued as far as Crossens.

When this service was opened in 1904 there were seventeen trains to and from Crossens each weekday. There was an hourly service through the day, with additional trains during the rush hours. The distance between Chapel Street station and Crossens station was three miles, and the journey lasted about eleven minutes.[1] The number of trains from Crossens to Southport each day rose to as many as fifty-two. The station's location on the southern fringe of the village reinforced the move of the centre of gravity of Crossens away from the area of The Plough.

Sewerage Scheme

Early in the twentieth century, the inadequacies of Southport's new sewerage scheme had been very publicly exposed. At the census of 1901, the population of Southport was still below that required for county borough status, which would have given the ambitious town enhanced local government powers. The absorption of Birkdale, which had its own Urban District Council, would have enabled Southport to attain the necessary population level. Birkdale had long resisted Southport's amalgamation overtures, but in 1903 Southport tried once again. One of the grounds for amalgamation that was argued by Southport at the Local Government Enquiry was the persistent failure of Birkdale Council to provide an adequate sewerage system. Birkdale's sewage disposal system used Fine Jane's Brook to carry treated waste to Crossens, and Southport had repeatedly accused Birkdale of contaminating this open '… water course running through or on the boundary of the Borough.' At the Enquiry, however, Southport's case was fatally damaged when the Rev. Bulpit criticised Southport's own drainage system. He complained that: '… the sewage effluent of Southport, which was discharged into the Crossens Pool Channel at a point right out on the foreshore was continually, by the incoming tides, being spread over the foreshore adjoining Crossens.'[2] Consequently, the Board judged that a local authority that could not efficiently manage its own waste disposal was not in a position to take responsibility for that of another, and amalgamation was again averted.

Southport's response to this rebuff was to attempt to put its own house in order. New sewerage works were built at Bank End and opened in 1907 (see rear endpaper). It was then claimed that the standard of purification of the waste was satisfactory for discharge into an inland river, let alone into tidal waters. Birkdale was still having difficulties in meeting its obligations to provide an efficient sewerage system and, rather than face the enormous expense which would be involved, it was finally decided to amalgamate with Southport and take advantage of its new facilities.[3] Despite the improvements at Bank End, however, there was still periodic fouling of the Pool Channel. One local tale concerning the condition of the water there involved Professor Bert Powsey, the professional diver, who performed off Southport Pier. He accepted a wager of ten shillings (50p) to dive into any water in the borough. His challenger specified the Pool at Crossens. Powsey made the dive into the filthy water and then, ignoring the comfort of his fellow passengers, caught a bus to Southport to have a hot tub at the Victoria Baths.

Fig. 63. Drawing of the new Vulcan factory 1906

Large Scale Industry

The introduction of an electric railway and opening of a new sewerage system were significant changes in this still rural community, but the new century was to see an even more dramatic event – the building of the Vulcan motor works. Two of four brothers from Leigh – Thomas and Joseph Hampson – had started the business in Southport, some six years earlier, in 1901. Thomas was previously employed at Bolton Technical College as the chief manual instructor. There, between 1897 and 1899, the brothers built an experimental car. (This was only two years after the Santler brothers had built the earliest English petrol-driven car.) Thomas and Joseph Hampson decided to launch a motor car building venture in Southport. It seems that they had three reasons for choosing this affluent and attractive seaside town. First, they believed that the residents included a number of potential customers. This proved to be true; wealthy Southport residents took quickly to the new form of transport and a very active motor club was formed. It also seemed likely that there was also a pool of potential investors. Much investment was made on a local basis at this time, and capital of some £10,000 was quickly raised. The brothers also accurately concluded that the area would be attractive to workers from industrial towns. In fact, some workers from Wigan and Bolton immediately followed them to Southport.

Fig. 64. Enlarged Vulcan works, post 1911. The original buildings can be seen on the right. This aerial photograph reveals the green field nature of the site. In the foreground is Crossens station with its extensive goods' sidings

The firm started in a building in Yellow House Lane, adjacent to the town-centre. Some early models had a tiller rather than a steering wheel. The Company expanded rapidly and moved to a former Volunteer drill hall, in what is now Vulcan Street, off Hawesside Road. It soon grew to employ 200 workers and declared an annual profit of £7,000. In 1906 a new company was formed, £63,000 capital was raised and the operation was moved to a new dedicated purpose-built factory, on a green field site at Crossens *(Fig. 63)*. A later aerial photograph shows it completely surrounded by fields, and there were no buildings between the factory and the sea. Critically, the site was alongside the railway station, thus affording ready access for workers from the town *(Fig. 64)*.

Opened in 1907, the factory was the first building that was met in Rufford Road, on crossing the railway bridge from Bankfield Lane. The elegantly windowed central office block was constructed in rich red pressed Accrington brick, in which the Company's name was picked out. An attractive cupola capped the building. Additional workshops were built in 1911, and the distinctive tall clock tower, with a steeply pitched slate roof, was added in 1913 *(Fig. 65)*. The tower contained the factory's large water tank. This was

Fig. 65. Vulcan power house and the clock tower

Fig. 66. Vulcan machine shop

83

Southport's only major factory, and Bulpit aptly described it as an 'exotic' in Crossens.[4] The arrival of a building of this size and quality, and the apparent prosperity of the firm must have given a great boost to the area. The fine image was not restricted to the exterior of the factory; the workshops were fitted with modern electrically operated machinery *(Fig. 66)*, and the electricity was generated in the Vulcan's own powerhouse.

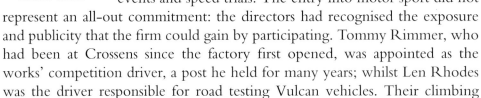

The first year at Crossens was, however, to be traumatic and a loss of £4,000 was sustained on the increased capital. Dissatisfied shareholders queried the veracity of the accounts. It was claimed that the recorded stock included a large quantity of costly but relatively worthless scrap castings. Part of the business was still being conducted at Hawesside Street, and shortly after the annual general meeting a fire gutted the painting and finishing shop there, reducing fifty-seven cars to scrap. Thomas Hampson had visited the factory late on the evening of the fire, but had left shortly before the outbreak was discovered. Fortunately for the firm the damage, which was estimated at £4,000, was covered by insurance.[5]

Vulcan cars, particularly the fourteen-horsepower model, were popular with motorists. The factory also produced racing models to take part in tourist trophy events and speed trials. The entry into motor sport did not represent an all-out commitment: the directors had recognised the exposure and publicity that the firm could gain by participating. Tommy Rimmer, who had been at Crossens since the factory first opened, was appointed as the works' competition driver, a post he held for many years; whilst Len Rhodes was the driver responsible for road testing Vulcan vehicles. Their climbing capability was tested on Parbold Hill.

Fig. 67. Vulcan radiator mascot

In 1910 the Vulcan's famous radiator mascot of a blacksmith at his forge was introduced to the marque (Vulcan was the Roman God of fire) *(Fig. 67)*. The Company adopted the marketing slogan – 'Ask the man who owns one'. A two-cylinder Vulcan ten-horsepower model was said to have been the '… sensation of the world-famous Crystal Palace Show.'[6] An ability to put cars on the market at what were considered to be reasonable prices was a feature of the Company. Vulcan had agents in at least eleven foreign countries. A 1910 Vulcan car is now included in the Liverpool Museum collection. It is possibly unique in that it is the only known surviving example of a Doctor's Phaeton model, which allowed the owner, often a doctor, to store extra

Fig. 68. Vulcan cars came in all shapes and sizes

belongings under his seat. Another larger model took its name from a fashionable suburb of Southport – a Birkdale Landaulet. The immediate pre-World War One period was the most prosperous time in the Company's history, although the policy of building such a wide range of vehicles would generate problems later *(Fig. 68)*. In 1913 Vulcan launched a new concept in motoring, a 'baby car' which would be offered at the modest price of £100. Unfortunately, the onset of the war prevented the exploitation of this idea, which was later to have such an impact on the industry.

Despite its apparent engineering success, the Company experienced some commercially hard times. Nevertheless, the workforce was built up to some 700 workers. It appears that many of them lived in Crossens. The son of an early Vulcan worker later wrote that: '... the fact that one worked there gave one a certain cachet in the community.'[7] Billy Gordon, who was born in New Lane and worked at the Vulcan, later recalled that: 'The whole of New Lane was occupied by Vulcan workers, many of whom came to the village from other Lancashire towns.'[8] One such worker was Ernie Knowles. He was attracted to Crossens by the prospect of working at a new factory, which he judged to be '... years ahead of its time.' Working in light airy glass-roofed sheds, in a factory surrounded by fields was '... far removed from the industrial grime of Lancashire.'[9] Knowles worked himself up in the Company

85

Fig. 69. Aeroplane manufacture at Vulcan

to become an '… executive with responsibility for sales and service.' He then '… decided to buy a house, in a more fashionable area than Crossens', and moved to Manning Road, convenient for Meols Cop Station. It was an area where a number of Vulcan managers lived. Crossens did supply some executives for Vulcan. William Rimmer, whose father had farmed Copeland Farm, went to a private school, later obtained a professional qualification and became the company secretary.

As the factory had been built alongside the railway station, many Vulcan workers travelled to Crossens on the train *(see rear endpaper)*. W.R. Birchley recalled that he caught the crowded 5.40 am train from Southport Station on Chapel Street; further workers joined at the intermediate stations, and the porters had to '… push their human cargo tighter by closing the doors.'[10] Workers failing to get into the factory before the start of the six o'clock shift were 'locked out' until breakfast time at eight-thirty. It seems that there was a strict discipline regime within the factory; absence at the toilet beyond the permitted four minutes led to wages being docked. Nevertheless, the workforce appeared to have a high regard for their employer, and this loyalty to Vulcan was to persist long after the company had disappeared.

World War One saw a rapidly expanding order book as the factory moved into the production of lorries, gun limbers, ambulances and aeroplane parts.

Fig. 70. Vulcan football team

Vulcan prided itself in being the only factory in the country, outside existing aeroplane manufacturers, which was building warplanes. It produced all the parts, except the engine, for a number of aircraft, including the DH9 *(Fig. 69)*. The aeroplanes were assembled and then flown off from the Hesketh Road Aerodrome, where two brick and wood Belfast truss hangars had been built, and the beach acted as an airstrip.[11] Vulcan later made engines for other aeroplanes. Hampson's commitment to the war effort appeared to be total. From within his workforce he formed and started to train a military unit, complete with its own silver band, for which he bought the instruments. He encouraged his workers to enlist in the armed forces, but many of the volunteers were too old or unfit for service. Nevertheless, a number did join the colours and women were recruited to take on jobs in the factory. Hampson put £10,000 into War Loans and launched a scheme in which he subsidised participation by his workers. Vulcan workers paraded through the town, demonstrating the Company's large-scale involvement in production for the armed forces. Convalescing wounded soldiers were entertained at the factory and even a football team of girls was raised to play against them. The firm sponsored a number of organisations for its employees. It had a sports ground in Bankfield Lane, where the football team played *(Fig. 70)*. There was also a boxing club and the Vulcan-Hesketh Bowling Club.

Fig. 71. Celebrating the production of lorry chassis no. 1,000 in 1920 – The Vulcan silver band can be seen behind the vehicles

Much involved in public service, Thomas Hampson, a Conservative, became Mayor of Southport in 1917, and was the first Roman Catholic to hold the office. Shortly after the end of the war, however, he suddenly retired from the firm. The reason soon became evident – he was charged with embezzling some £22,000 of Company funds. Found guilty of what the judge described as '… a very bad fraud', a twelve-month jail sentence followed.[12] This was not the end of the Company's problems, although it certainly knew how to put on a brave face. The Vulcan had attempted to build on its wartime success, when it was producing over a hundred lorries a week, by moving into the large-scale production of lorries with the V.S.C. (the Vulcan Standard Commercial vehicle). Cyril Ralphs was the designer and he appears to have been responsible for the introduction of a wide range of specialist vehicles, based on a standard thirty hundredweight lorry chassis. In June 1920 the Company held a grand dinner at the Prince of Wales Hotel to celebrate the manufacture of over 1,000 lorry chassis in the first six months of the year *(Fig. 71)*. The Vulcan Silver Band played, under the baton of bandmaster Rawson, and one of the guests spoke of how '… directors, foremen, and employees shared a bond of brotherhood.'[13] Despite these confident words, however, less than two months later the workforce of approximately 2,000 was served with a week's notice. Sales of the lorry chassis had been sluggish and the firm was holding large stocks. The directors blamed government failure to prevent the import of lorries from the United States. They also pointed to the difficulty of recovering from the diversified production of the war years, particularly from the manufacture of aeroplanes and the consequent emphasis on making wooden airframes. They said that they would re-organize the factory for the production of a Vulcan Standard Pleasure Car before re-opening.[14] One of the problems that persisted at Vulcan was the number and variety of models which were produced. David Hales, (an historian of Vulcan vehicles) revealed the existence of more models than one might think possible for so small a company. In contrast, William Morris, using mass-production techniques, had produced and sold 54,000 'Bullnose' Morris models by 1925, thus making his Oxford-based company the country's largest car producer.

The changes at Vulcan were taking place against a background of continuing litigation involving the Hampson family. Joseph, the former works' manager and chief engineer who had been dismissed, was facing three charges of financial irregularity. The charges were withdrawn in an out-of-court settlement, although ambiguities in the agreement led to further legal disputes.[15] The motor trade was still sluggish and only a reduced workforce of about 1,000 was re-employed. Vulcan cars were hardly revolutionary in design. In fact, David Hales described them as '... fairly ordinary, but well executed and competitively priced.'[16] Another author described the cars as having a reputation for '... quality, reliability and longevity.'[17] Old Vulcan workers later told tales of industrial espionage at Crossens. It seems that, when visiting directors of car firms from the Midlands were being entertained for lunch at the Prince of Wales Hotel, the cars that they arrived in were furtively stripped down, examined and re-assembled in time for them to drive back.

Notwithstanding the management's efforts to re-establish the Company, all was not well and the board was coming under considerable pressure from its shareholders. In 1921, the factory was again closed down '...because of trade depression', and the vast majority of the workforce was laid off, the men being told that they would be re-engaged as required.[18] The management then sought to reduce the wages and to increase the hours worked each week. The unions decided to resist the proposals, but meantime some creditors served a winding-up order on the firm. The Company continued to exhibit a brave face. The *Southport Visiter* reported an order from the War Office for fifty lorries, which was fulfilled within a week. Vulcan attempted to achieve some degree of rationalisation in the range of cars that it produced, and concentrated on building a standard twelve horsepower model. It was claimed

"THE MOTOR," January 4, 1925.

A LADY'S IDEAL CAR.

4ᴰ

THE
VULCAN
"TWELVE"
Standard Saloon - Price £395
Latest Catalogue Free.
The VULCAN Motor & Engineering
Co. (1906) Ltd., SOUTHPORT.
LONDON.
VULCAN MOTORS (LONDON), LTD.,
118-137, Great Portland Street, W.1.
See Advertisement in this issue.

TRAVEL WITH COMFORT THROUGH 1925.

Fig. 72. The Vulcan Standard Saloon 1925

that 599 of these cars had been sold at the Olympia Motor Show, and orders taken for the immediate delivery of another hundred. In a review in *The Autocar* magazine, the author later described this family car, which sold at £395, as being '… offered at a moderate figure and possessed of a credible road perform-ance.' It was a car that he judged to be competitively priced and worthy of '… close study.'[19] Buoyed by the efforts of the Company to improve its position, a majority of the creditors agreed to a rescue scheme. The High Court judge hearing the winding-up petition concurred with the majority, and Vulcan continued to trade.

From 1922, Vulcan worked with Lea-Francis of Coventry. Both firms were hoping that this '… liaison … would provide the open sesame to a successful future.'[20] The firms pooled dealerships and rationalised some of their production, with Lea-Francis making the gearboxes and steering gear for the cars. The result was that both firms ended up with a car on which only the wheels and the badge were substantially different. By 1924, the Vulcan's turnover had increased, more men were employed, but there had not yet been a complete recovery.[21] Nevertheless, such was the demand for motor cars that a night shift was re-introduced and the workforce expanded to 1,225.[22] The management claimed that, within three hours of opening at the Olympia Motor Exhibition, they had received orders for 1,500 vehicles with a value of more than £600,000 *(Fig. 72)*. It was suggested that much of this trade was with Australia and New Zealand, where British manufactured goods still enjoyed the protection of 'Imperial Preference'. The company reported an increase of seventy per cent in overseas sales. Such was the improvement in its fortunes, that in 1925 it was able to report a net profit of £1,097. This was after having paid interest on the two previous years' losses of £88,805.[23] The net profit for the following year was £18,963 and the Company's liabilities had been reduced by £40,990. The Chairman reported that the export

90

Fig. 73. Building Vulcan bus bodies

business was firmly established and continued to expand.[24] Enterprise and opportunism characterised Vulcan marketing. The annual net profit again increased and the debt decreased, causing an editorial in the *Southport Visiter* to describe the transformation as the '… most remarkable in the history of the motor industry in this country.'[25]

The reality again failed to match the hyperbole and, anxious to find a winning formula, Vulcan experimented with buses. Its first was produced in 1924, and the firm built the first single-deckers for the Southport Corporation. Despite this initiative, the Company's problems persisted: in December 1927 there was again a temporary closure of the factory, and the workforce of over 1,000 was trimmed to half of this size. In the following year, the production of cars was finally stopped and Vulcan concentrated solely on twenty and thirty-two seater buses and commercial vehicles *(Fig. 73)*. Although a new board of directors was introduced, the Company's financial problems continued, and three years later the Tilling Stevens group acquired the manufacturing rights to build Vulcan cars in Maidstone. Rootes then acquired Tilling Stevens and the Vulcan motor marque disappeared.

The Crossens works appears to have become largely a body shop for commercial vehicles, including buses. At a time when authorities were changing from single-decker buses to double-decker vehicles, Vulcan

91

Fig. 74. A Crossens washerwoman

introduced their fifty-one seater 'Emperor'. It was claimed that a new Vulcan '... Monarch engine was developed and built for these vehicles, at Crossens.'[26] Letters to local papers urged the Southport Corporation to purchase some 'Emperors'. An 'Emperor' was displayed on Lord Street, in an attempt to attract public support. Although the Corporation was also giving a trial to a Leyland bus, a Vulcan was purchased. More substantial orders came from the Birmingham and other local authorities, leading to additional workers being employed.[27] It seems that there were quite serious, if unsuccessful, negotiations for the take-over of the Vulcan factory by the Leyland Company, geographically a relatively close neighbour.[28] Some relief for the Company came when Southport Corporation then ordered fourteen of the 'Emperors'. In 1937, however, the Company failed to secure a contract from the Southport Corporation to build the bodies for five further double-decker buses. The contract went to a firm which quoted a price nine per cent lower than that of Vulcan.[29] Protests from union officials representing some 250 vehicle builders and sheet metal workers, who lived in the town, came to naught and in the following year the factory was acquired by J. Brockhouse Engineering Ltd., a firm from the Midlands. It is interesting to note that after his term in gaol, Tom Hampson, a founder of the Vulcan Company, joined the Board of Brockhouse. He rose to the position of General Manager, and was responsible for the Company acquiring the run-down remnants of the Vulcan Motor Company.[30]

Early in the century, industrial work for women had also arrived in Crossens with the opening of the Ideal Laundry about 1912. Mechanisation had replaced the 'washerwoman', a female occupation which had been common in Crossens. The 1901 census enumerators' returns show no fewer than forty women and girls engaged in this work *(Fig. 74)*. Urban Southport created work for several laundries and they tended to be situated on the outer fringes of the town. Their coal-fired boilers were potential sources of

Fig. 75. An Ideal Laundry delivery van. The laundry is in the background

pollution, and the amount of wastewater created was often too great for the drains to cope with. Where residential property developed close to one of the laundries, as in Birkdale, complaints about the smoke and flood 'nuisance' became very common. The Ideal Laundry was at the inland end of Brook Street *(see rear endpaper)*. Efficient drainage to Fine Jane's Brook and thus to the Sluice must have been easy to achieve. The prevailing south-westerly winds would have carried the smoke from the laundry's tall chimney out over the Mere. Being located on the edge of the built-up area, the firm was able to boast of having 'extensive open-air drying grounds', and being: 'The laundry in the fields' *(Fig. 75)*. In 1924, the proprietor – Councillor G.H. Hibbott – installed a giant water softener, which could process 24,000 gallons of Southport's notoriously hard water, from the deep wells at Scarisbrick, each day, to enable the wash to be done with the 'Purest Soft Water'. In the 1920s the Ideal employed some forty, mostly long-serving, women. Relationships between management and workers appear to have been harmonious. In fact, at a time of industrial agitation, a number of the workers wrote to the local paper claiming that: 'Laundry girls are as happy and contented as anyone else.'[31] Further jobs for women arrived in the 1930s with the Stirling Knitting Factory, which was built on Rufford Road, alongside the Vulcan.

Southport residents' perceptions of Crossens were coloured by its industrial dimension and its role as the location of the town's sewerage works. It is not surprising that when there were local objections to '... the intolerable smell' of a new Corporation bitumen plant in Forrest Road, it was suggested that it should be re-sited in Crossens.[32] In describing his Southport Town Planning Plan in 1924, A.E. Jackson, the Borough Engineer, wrote of:

> Areas of the town where industries are permitted ... They are at the outskirts of the town, at Crossens, Blowick, and between Liverpool Road and the eastern boundary. These positions are placed to the leeward of the town, taking into consideration the prevailing winds.[33]

Confirmation of the Corporation's intentions at Crossens was revealed in a regional town-planning venture. A consortium of nineteen local authorities formed the South West Lancashire Joint Town Planning Advisory Committee. In its plan – *The Future Development of South West Lancashire* – produced in 1930, it recommended that the whole of Crossens from Blundells Lane to the sea (except for the existing housing in and around Rufford Road) should be '... zoned for industry.'[34] That would have been all the land on both sides of the Crossens section of Preston New Road.

Agriculture and Fishing

One local councillor described Crossens in 1933 as '... one of the few industrial neighbourhoods of Southport ', and expressed the hope that it would '... also retain its rich tradition as an agricultural village.'[35] In fact, as late as 1930 there were still nine working farms within half a mile of St. John's.[36] The Scarisbrick family owned most of the agricultural land around Crossens and did not hesitate to take their farm tenants to court where damage was caused by '... the failure to cultivate the land according to the rules of good husbandry.'[37] Bill Langden succeeded Mayor as the estate's head keeper. Local directories show that all the old nineteenth-century farms were still active. In Rufford Road, Hugh Ainscough was at Hey's Farm, John Ball, the agricultural contractor, at Plough Farm, Paul Cropper at Causeway, Richard Gregson at Johnson's, and James Sutton at Barton's; whilst in Banks Road Jos Aughton was at Aughton Farm, Barnaby Rimmer at Rectory and Thomas Rimmer at Copeland. Many of these families had farmed these lands for generations. In addition, Thomas Cropper, Thomas Howard, David Howard, Edward Neale, James Wareing and Thomas Wright were also listed as farmers. The surviving farms were larger, and on the whole the farmers more prosperous than their nineteenth-century predecessors.

Fig. 76. Hawking farm produce outside The Plough

Potatoes, spring wheat, oats and hay were still a typical rotation of crops for Crossens' farmers. Cows and sheep grazed the meadows and marshes. Poultry farms, to provide fresh eggs and birds, had become a feature on the fringes of conurbations, and areas with easy transport links to markets. The first to appear in Crossens was that of John Sutton in New Lane followed by that of George Dixon in Banks Road. Being on the rural fringe of Southport, there were a number of dairies in Crossens. There was a long local tradition of farmers hawking their produce locally, particularly on Saturdays *(Fig. 76)*.

Southport had boasted a deep-sea fishing fleet of some eighty smacks at the end of the nineteenth century. The progressive silting of the offshore channels caused the remnants of this fleet to finally quit its pier-head anchorage, in the late 1920s. The majority of local fishermen changed to using a horse and cart for inshore shrimping; whilst a few continued to operate in boats from Crossens Pool. In 1933, Richard Rimmer, a fisherman from Crossens, claimed that the fleet was down to seven boats, and that these boats were anchored three and a half miles out, at a sandbank at the mouth of the Crossens Pool Channel.[38] The building of embankments to reclaim land impaired the outlet of this channel. Accretion made it difficult for the waters to force their way over the flat land to the sea. The larger boats of the original

Fig. 77. Shallow-draught fishing boats. In the right background the pumping station and in the centre the stone 'Quay Nook', Crossens' old harbour

fishing fleet were sold off and a handful of smaller shallow-draught boats continued to use the Pool *(Fig. 77)*.[39] Nevertheless, the age-old reluctance of the local residents to fish persisted, and few men from Crossens were involved.

The shallow meandering Pool Channel needed regular and expensive dredging. Under the Land Drainage Act of 1930 The Crossens Catchment Drainage Board had been set up and Tom Booth, who worked for the Scarisbrick Trust, was appointed as Works' Superintendent to the new Board.[40] It seems that the men working for the Board were permitted to smoke '… owing to the offensive nature of the material excavated from the brooks.'[41] In 1933, the ageing steam engines in the pumping station were replaced with three new diesel pumps. Nine years later, the Catchment Board undertook a £8,000 scheme to store water in reservoirs, when the tide prevented the gates opening to release it. It was hoped that the scheme would help to prevent some 4,000 acres becoming waterlogged. The majority of the coarse fishing rights in the channels leading to Crossens were held by the Southport and District Angling Association, and in 1927 twenty members went to a richly stocked pool in Cheshire, caught some 1,500 fish and brought them back for release in the Sluice.[42]

Fig. 78. Rufford Road – the new centre of the village. The tall roofs of the two Methodist chapels can be seen on the left and the tower of St. John's on the right

The Village

Although the open space in front of The Plough was the historical centre of the village, there was a shift of balance in the early twentieth century. The introduction of industry to Crossens, along with the siting of the railway station at the southern boundary, and the building of further houses led to Rufford Road becoming the centre of the village. It had become a small neighbourhood shopping centre and was the location of St. John's church, the school, and the two popular Methodist chapels *(Fig. 78 & rear endpaper)*. The siting of the Post Office brought this issue to the surface. One correspondent to the *Southport Visiter* wrote: 'Truly the centre is now nearer New Lane.' He went on to ask '… what about the top end of the village', and suggested that there ought to be a pillar-box with an automatic stamp machine attached there.[43] The ornamental house alongside St. John's School became the local police office, with a small lock-up at the rear *(Fig. 79)*. Early in the century William Forbes was the resident constable, later, through the 1920s and into the 1930s, Edward Pardoe Hall held the office.

Southport became a County Borough in 1905. It appears, however, that the residents of Crossens tended to feel rather neglected and on the fringe of municipal concerns. At the Festival of 1925 the vicar, the Rev.

Fig. 79. 198 Rufford Road – the police office

W.M. Larcombe, reminded guests, including the Mayor of Southport, that: 'Crossens was part of the borough.'[44] Crossens councillors campaigned vigorously on behalf of their village. Perhaps one of the most active was a radical, Councillor Hibbott, the proprietor of the Ideal Laundry. In the 1920s, he pressed for both a bus service for Crossens and better postal and telephone services. There were no mail collections at the weekend and the only available public telephone was inside the Post Office. He also campaigned for a recreation ground, a bowling green and a library. He ran well-attended public meetings, organised petitions and never lost an opportunity to speak on behalf of the village. In 1927 he used his year as mayor to try to raise the profile of Crossens. But, in the following year, the newly installed vicar of St. John's again warned the Southport Corporation that '… it would have to look to its laurels or else the Crossens people would continue their criticisms.'[45] A speaker at the Horticultural Show in the following year suggested that: 'If Crossens is not provided with a bowling green in the next few years, he will be a brave councillor who dares to go into the village.'[46]

The return of ex-servicemen from World War One was a significant factor in persuading the Southport Council to finally address the problem of providing sound cheap housing for the working classes, an issue that had been consistently ignored by the landowners and the local authority. The availability of financial help from the government, under the Housing and Town Planning Act of 1919, partially explains this change in policy. The Town Planning Committee opted for '… small pairs of detached houses of good design in well laid out streets.'[47]

The Corporation had two prongs to its 1920 housing thrust in Crossens. It used its own workforce to build two pairs of traditional pebble-dashed semi-detached houses. These were built at a cost of £1,000 each, which it was claimed constituted a saving of some £250 on each house. In addition to these houses, built by direct labour, the Corporation placed a contract for the building of eighty-four houses by an outside firm, the Unit Production Company, a national builder, which was working on schemes throughout the United Kingdom. The firm was applying mass-production techniques to house-building, deploying separate specialist teams to prepare the site, lay the foundations, set the blocks, make the roofs, and to fit the houses out. The houses were built of large blocks, which were manufactured on site from cement and crushed stone. They were well spaced out and the layout included small cul-de-sacs. Two sizes of houses were offered: the smaller had a living room, hall, scullery, bathroom and three bedrooms; whilst the larger houses also had a parlour and a fourth bedroom. It was decided that the majority of those built in Crossens should be of the smaller kind and that the rent should be 12s 6d (62.5p) per week. Before they were built, the Corporation had already received 515 applications for the houses in Crossens. An estate was developed around North Road and Ribble Avenue *(Figs. 80 & 81)*. It joined Brade Street to form a loop off Rufford Road, further reinforcing the emerging dominance of this end of the village *(see rear endpaper)*. Significantly, the junction of North Road with Rufford Road became the terminus of the bus service to Crossens. This junction was also to become the location of Crossens' first public telephone kiosk. It was a distinctive structure, made from reinforced concrete and topped with decorative ironwork and a spike.

In addition to the Corporation housing initiative there was a Vulcan scheme to build twenty-five semi-detached houses, on a site opposite to the factory, now The Crescent. A society was formed in the works, with a committee of representatives of the management and workers. Shares were issued for this government-assisted scheme under which the workers would be able to rent or buy a house. The 1920 slow-down at Vulcan created an atmosphere of uncertainty. As a result, there was no longer a demand from workers for these houses. The Society offered to sell them to the Corporation. They had been completed much more quickly than the local authority's block houses and were offered at a hundred pounds each less; nevertheless, the Corporation refused to buy them and left the Society to dispose of them on the open market.

By the end of 1921 all the Corporation houses at Crossens had been completed and allocated to tenants, with the majority of them being rented. In fact only one was sold. It seems that the purchaser would soon have cause to regret his decision, as the value of property was to plummet and the cost of building a comparable house eighteen months later fell by two-thirds. In 1923, the Corporation decided to build twenty-eight small houses in Crossens, on the remainder of the land that had originally been bought with

Fig 80. Newly-built council houses in North Road

Fig. 81. Ribble Avenue

Fig. 82. Elizabeth Tomlinson talking to a distinguished looking visitor outside her shop on Banks Road

Government subsidy under the Housing Act. Later in the year there was a further change in policy, and the Corporation obtained permission to sell the last sixteen plots to private developers. The small houses built in Pool Street, Brook Street and Land Lane were still subject to the Government subsidy.[48] As council house building developed in Southport, the focus moved away from Crossens to building large estates on green field sites at Birkdale.

Private builders enjoyed only limited success in adding to the housing stock of Crossens during this period. Minutes of the Corporation Estates Committee show that planning permission for houses was given to a number of companies, but few houses were built. G.H. Ball, a local builder, was given approval for 158 houses in 1933. The site, off North Road, included Roselea Drive and Holmdale Avenue. Building started in Holmdale Avenue in 1934 and several houses were built, but the development was not completed and the road and pavements remained unmade. There were no street lamps, and this damp muddy area, alongside the line of the old 'Pool', was riddled with deep potholes and attracted the name of the 'Lake District'.[49]

Although this expanding suburb was quite well provided with shops it did not initially attract professional services. There was no doctor's surgery, but a Maternity and Infant Welfare Centre and a chemist's shop (John Hodgson's) were opened in Rufford Road in the early 1920s. Previously, the 1901 census

Fig. 83. Jane Tomlinson poses for her brother's camera

returns showed a midwife – the sixty-six-year-old wife of a corporation labourer – as the only medical support listed in the village. By 1939 there was a doctor's surgery (Dr. C.G.J. Rayner) in Rufford Road.

One of Crossens' commercially successful families was the Tomlinsons, of The Plough. In addition to his son Henry, who succeeded him in the business, John had five daughters. One of these – Elizabeth – kept a small grocery shop in Banks Road, which later embraced the sale of drapery *(Fig. 82)*. Elizabeth emigrated to America with her sister Jane, a milliner, who had helped her in the shop *(Fig. 83)*. Henry was an enthusiastic amateur photographer, owning a number of cameras. He was an active member of the Southport Photographic Society, and frequently gave 'magic lantern' shows at St. John's Institute and around the district. Fortunately, a large number of his glass negatives and slides have been preserved, and prints from many of them appear in this book.

Part of the Dock Lane Bank (Rossall Men's Bank), an old sea-wall that had been superseded by the 1892 sea-bank, later had to be demolished to make way for the building of Preston New Road *(see rear endpaper)*. This new seventy-five-feet-wide main road from Southport by-passed Crossens, with its narrow winding Rufford Road and high rail bridge. Road safety was a major factor in its provision, but the timing was partially determined by the anxiety to relieve the current unemployment.[50] The Ministry of Labour paid a half of the £44,000 that the road cost. An old cottage, at the junction of Dock Lane and Rufford Road, had to be demolished *(Fig. 84)*. In the absence of an official ceremony to mark the opening in 1925, the people of Marshside, which was at the southern end of the one and a quarter-mile-long road, decided that the honours should be done by eighty-year-old Nicholas (Manty) Wright, one of the community's oldest and most respected fishermen. The ceremony involved him riding his tricycle and cutting a rope at both ends of the road.[51] The new road, with a 150-feet-wide gap between

Fig. 84. Cottage at the corner of Rufford Road and Dock Lane

the building lines, also had the potential to open up the area for housing, but this was not initially realised. Miss Ormrod, a young teacher in St. John's Infant School in the mid 1930s, travelled to Crossens by bus from Southport each day and recalls that there were few houses on the Crossens end of Preston New Road. There was a second bus route along Bankfield Lane and Miss Ormrod suggests that there, too, there was quite a gap separating Crossens from Churchtown. She claimed that these gaps helped to give Crossens '… very much a village feel, not that of a suburb.'[52]

The Landowners

Sir Charles Scarisbrick, whom the vicar of St. John's described as '… a good friend of the people of Crossens',[53] died in 1923, and was interred alongside his wife in the family mausoleum. After the death of his father, Charles' son Thomas Talbot Scarisbrick relinquished Greaves Hall, which he had built at Banks, and moved to the ancient family home at Scarisbrick Hall, which he had purchased in 1923 from one of the de Castejas, who had inherited it. Evidence of his continuing links with Crossens came in 1924, when he entertained a party of eighty adults from St. John's at Scarisbrick Hall. At the tea, after a tour of the house and gardens, he expressed his pleasure at renewing '… acquaintance with several old friends.'[54] At a church function in

1925, Mr. Brookfield said that: 'Ever since I was a boy, the name of Scarisbrick had been a household word in Crossens.'[55] In the same year, Sir Thomas was instrumental in dismantling the Scarisbrick Trust, and having the estate divided between the three families who were the beneficiaries. He then set about disposing of his share, although retaining Scarisbrick Hall. Such sales of assets were a common practice with many landowners at this time: in fact, in 1927, Charles Hesketh Bibby Fleetwood-Hesketh sold most of his holdings in North Meols to the Hesketh Estate Company. Thomas Talbot Scarisbrick died in 1933 and his son Everard, who lived at Scarisbrick Hall, identified with the immediate surrounding area. Unlike his father and grandfather, he does not appear to have been closely involved with the Crossens community. When the Trust was divided in 1925, some of the land around Crossens went to the Naylor Leyland branch of the Scarisbrick family. Charles Scarisbrick's daughter Mary Ann had married Thomas Naylor Leyland, of the Naylor Leyland family, who were baronets and knights with estates in Northampton and North Wales. Members of this family were rarely seen in Southport.

Religion, Education and Recreation

The Rev. Bulpit retired in 1904, after twenty-six years of service in Crossens, and died in 1914. He was buried at St. John's and his wife presented a brass lectern, of the popular eagle pattern, to mark his memory. The fact that his pension had been paid out of the next vicar's stipend was one of the reasons why his successor the Rev. Z. Edwards moved on after a relatively short stay at Crossens. Edwards achieved some local notoriety by disguising himself as a tramp, in an attempt to share their hardship and to experience their sense of rejection. He told his much-publicised story in a short pamphlet, *A Vicar as Vagrant*.[56]

It appears that St. John's Church was prospering, as the village expanded. One of the tasks facing it was attending to the organ, which had been bought second-hand when the church was rebuilt in the 1880s. The rebuilding of the organ, the installation of electric lights, and the redecoration of part of the interior marked the incumbency of the popular Rev. M.W. Larcombe. The Mayor described the church as '... a live church which stands for a great deal in Crossens.'[57] Further Scarisbrick support for the church living was a gift by Sir Charles of the ground rents for several cottages. A leading character at St. John's was 'Mester Johnson' – James Johnson of Banks Road. He was sexton between 1897 and 1928, and after relinquishing these duties the congregation bought him an invalid tricycle and he continued to act as the church caretaker. In 1937, Larcombe's successor, the Rev. W.V. Walmsley, wrote a short history to commemorate the church's centenary.[58] Oddly, although the Scarisbrick mausoleum dominates the churchyard, and the Scarisbrick family had been significant benefactors for the church, Walmsley chose to ignore its presence.

Many of the divisions that existed between the various strands of Methodism were healed at a national uniting conference in 1932, and national unity came in 1933. In Crossens, however, the neighbouring United and Primitive Methodist chapels initially continued their separate existence. The *Southport North Circuit Plan* rather clumsily referred to them as Crossens ex U.M. and Crossens ex P.M. The congregations finally amalgamated, using the United Methodist Buildings. A separate congregation continued to meet in the former Primitive Methodist building, which became known as the Bethel Methodist Chapel. Both Methodist chapels had a number of outstanding stalwarts. Robert Marshall was the superintendent of the Primitive Methodist Sunday School for over forty years. During the years of the Second World War, the Methodist chapel appointed a talented young sixteen-year-old, Kenneth Blundell, as organist. His singing was also of such quality that he broadcast for the B.B.C.

St. John's was an all-age village elementary school, and the vast majority of its pupils completed their schooling there. The report on a government inspection, in 1923, said that:

> There is a bright and pleasant atmosphere about this little school. The teachers are energetic and enthusiastic, and the children evidently enjoy their lessons… The tone throughout is very good.[59]

Early in the century, many parents, particularly farming families, would seek a 'labour certificate' to allow their children to leave school early, in order to start work in the fields. By the 1920s, the occupation of leavers' statistics, in the *Southport Education Committee Yearbooks,* show no former pupils from St. John's going into farming.[60] Being apprenticed to a trade was the destination of the majority of the boys; whilst for girls, retail work, dressmaking and millinery, had overtaken the former dominant activity – 'helping at home'.

A major feature of Crossens village life in the twentieth century was the emergence of the annual Rose Queen celebrations. These were first held in 1906 on the second day of the Agricultural Show, although the Summer Festival was later held independently of this function. Originally instituted by St. John's, a village tradition was soon established and chapel and church children joined in together. The inaugural Rose Queen was Jennie Wareing, and a feature of the early festivals was the Rose Queen riding side-saddle on

Fig. 85. The Festival Queen on her horse 1907

a decorated horse at the head of the parade. Mr. Rimmer of Bridge Farm provided the horse for Queen Jennie *(Fig. 85)*. Banks Brass Band normally provided music for the parade, which included decorated wagons for the younger children, and maypole dancing *(Fig. 86)*. In 1910 a village wedding was added to the celebrations *(Fig. 87)*. In the same year Miss Burnley, the headmistress of the infants' school, introduced Morris dancing. She brought a group from Bolton and thereafter teams of Crossens boys, many trained by Tom Johnson, performed up until 1960. The custom of the queen riding a horse was discontinued in 1912, after Elsie Cropper had been thrown. It seems that:

> The procession had stopped. The band had stopped and the horse had stopped. But a page, with a hat that sported a long feather kept on walking… the feather brushed against the horse, up it reared and down slid Elsie.[61]

The festival was discontinued during World War One, but peace was celebrated in 1919 by the longest procession ever. A feature was the Peace Queen – Agnes Watkinson. As time passed the festival was refined and queens representing the four seasons of the year were introduced. Their fellow scholars at St. John's School elected the queens. The festival was the focus for

Fig. 86. Maypole dancers 1906

Fig. 87. Village wedding 1913

Fig. 88. Stalls had to be manned 1907

much activity within the community: the training and dressing of the children; making the floats and decorating the horses; and setting up the showground and manning the stalls *(Fig. 88)*. The event with the crowning of the queen, the village wedding and dance demonstrations by the children drew large crowds. Adults were charged a shilling (5p) and children half price. Additional trains were run from Southport to cope with the crowd. In the early years the festival was followed by sports, in which there were races for all the children who had taken part in the procession. A fancy dress turn-out later became an integral part of the festival.

Crossens' sense of being a village was reinforced by the emergence of strong sports clubs. These were identified very closely with the local community and enjoyed considerable playing success. Crossens Football Club was playing in the Southport and District Football League. Reaching the final of the Victory Cup in 1921, the match against High Park, played at the Ash Lane ground, attracted a crowd of some 3,000. Crossens' successes continued and in the 1925-1926 season the Club achieved a unique treble. Not only did it win the league championship, but also the two knock-out competitions. Crossens Juniors also enjoyed success and in the following year achieved a cup and league double. Crossens United Methodists had a junior team playing in the same league. At the Football Club's annual general meeting in 1928, the chairman stated that: 'It is the committee's desire to give due precedence to players residing in the village.'[62] The football club played at a sports field in New Lane *(see rear endpaper)*. Success on the field of play was matched with an improvement in facilities. Players had changed in the Institute, attached to the school, but in 1921 new dressing rooms were built at New Lane.

In 1923 a Crossens Cricket Club was formed. The team was placed in the Third Division of the Southport and District Amateur Cricket League. Playing at New Lane, the team dominated its league and ended the first season as champions, thus earning promotion to the Second Division. The team topped the Second Division and was promoted to Division One, and a second team was entered into the Fourth Division. 1924 had seen the formation of a multi-sport Crossens Club with its ground at New Lane. A new pavilion, complete with a tea-room, was built in 1927. During the war years Crossens Cricket Club, led by the free-scoring Bill Bithell, dominated the local league.

The Institute continued to prosper. The introduction of two full-size billiard tables proved to be popular with the members, and a team was entered in the Southport and District Institute Billiards League. It was in the early 1920s that a rowing club was formed at St. John's Sunday School. The club had two crews competing in the Southport Sunday School Rowing Association events and in its first year one of the crews, the Bond brothers – Arthur and John – won the Junior Cup. The club became a dominant force in the association. From the 1920s St. John's also had a lawn tennis club, whose courts were at New Lane. Further social provision took the form of a guide company and brownies for girls, under their Captain Bessie Critchley, and a scout troop and cubs for boys under scoutmaster Pilling. All four groups were attached to St. John's.

Prior to World War One, the village had some land for youngsters to use as a recreation ground. Under 'Defence of the Realm' regulations this land was partitioned into allotments, and in 1922 was still being used for this purpose. The nine acres for Crossens Recreation Ground were purchased in 1924, although it was as late as 1930 before the approach from Rufford Road was laid out, prior to the official opening. The bowlers had to wait until 1936 before a bowling green was finally added, after the submission of a petition from sixty local residents. A pavilion and toilets were also built for the bowlers. It seems that there was no bowling club at this time, although a petition in 1940 shows that there was a self-styled group of '... regular players at the Crossens Bowling Green.'[63]

The local authority had plans to open a reading room in the late 1920s. Originally it was intended that it should be in Brade Street, but the plots were built on. It was then decided to build it on the approach to the Recreation Ground. The cost was agreed at £3,000, but this was later amended to £2,000 and Crossens Reading Room, with newspapers, periodicals, reference books and some children's literature, was opened in 1931. The reading room was subsequently converted into a lending library service in 1942.

Some Memories of World War Two

With the advent of World War Two, Brockhouse Engineering was quickly into production for the armed forces. The workforce expanded to exceed 5,000, and the work included the manufacture, maintenance and repair of aircraft turrets and anti-aircraft guns. Bill Jaegar, an ex-tram and bus driver, later recalled having to undertake '... compulsory overtime to transport round-the-clock shift workers to Brockhouse Engineering Works.'[64] Further extensions were added to the factory at Crossens, but some work was also undertaken off-site at unlikely venues. The Scala Cinema on Kingsway and The Grand on Lord Street were both used. An employee – Arthur Knowles, the son of Ernie the former Vulcan Sales Manager – wrote a small book, *The Thoughts of a Machine Tool Setter,* based on his wartime experience in the factory. [65] In this book, the problems of a skilled engineer working with unskilled machinists and women, who formed the majority of the wartime workforce, are discussed. He later successfully pursued a career as a motoring correspondent and author. Having been immersed in the Vulcan ethos from childhood he was not an admirer of the Brockhouse Company. Later, in his autobiography, he wrote that: 'The place had changed, and the old atmosphere gone, to be replaced by something vaguely and indefinably unpleasant.'[66]

Brockhouse appears to have benefited from having been the solitary large factory in a residential town, and suffered little from air raids. The only bombing occurred in the autumn of 1940. Albert Evason, a Brockhouse worker who was a veteran of the early years of Vulcan, told the story to the *Southport Visiter* at a much later date. Censorship prevented contemporary newspapers from reporting such attacks. It seems that Southport was on the northern approach flight path for German bombers attacking Liverpool. It was speculated that the pilot of a twin-engined Dornier bomber had seen the glow from the firebox of a railway engine at Crossens and attempted to bomb the train. Inadvertently he hit the factory, which was not his target. An explosion in a tool room killed one lathe operative and injured others. A second bomb dropped in an assembly shop, but failed to explode. Its two-foot tall tail fin

Fig. 89. Tail-plane of a Junkers 88 bomber. This plane was shot down on Banks Marsh 7th April 1941

was kept in the factory as a souvenir of the incident. A former Brockhouse worker, George Wall of York Road, later kept it. A third bomb completely destroyed the adjacent stocking factory; whilst a fourth bomb blew up the grocery shop at the corner of The Crescent.[67]

Wartime production at Brockhouse meant a vastly increased work force. Not surprisingly, the Company spawned an array of social, cultural and sporting groups. There were monthly staff dances; whilst work for War Comforts and charity loomed large in the Brockhouse calendar. The factory had a musical society, an orchestra, a choir, a dramatic society and a camera club. In addition, there were football and cricket teams playing in the local leagues; men's and mixed hockey teams, a bowling section, a well-organised golf club, which had been playing at the Old Links since the 1920s, and a swimming club which held an annual gala; whilst the annual sports day was a popular event.

The war also saw the formation of the Local Defence Volunteers, which later became the Home Guard – 'Dads' Army'. Crossens D1 Platoon of the Southport Battalion was energetically led by Major J.E. Lapes. Serving in this platoon was lance corporal Jack Sawbridge, Crossens Cricket Club's outstanding bowler and the dominant figure in the Home Guard Annual

Sports. The platoon held regular exercises, with the Banks platoon frequently acting as the enemy. The 1941 crash of a shot down Junkers 88 on Banks Marsh was probably the nearest that the platoon came to seeing action *(Fig. 89)*. Two Allied planes came down in Crossens during the war. A Walrus seaplane crashed through a field fence on Preston New Road, close to where Hugh Gregson was delivering newspapers; and a Spitfire, from the Polish squadron stationed at Woodvale, crashed in fog down New Lane. David Gregson, Hugh's brother, recalls that fighter planes regularly took part in target practice over the marsh, and that the local youngsters later searched for souvenirs of these firing exercises. There was a special police post located alongside the old pumping station at the Sluice Bridge, which was responsible for informing fishermen when these exercises were to take place and when the Fairhaven battery, which guarded the Ribble estuary, was to fire practice rounds. Two bombs, which fell on the recreation ground, created a new amenity – a sand-pit.

The iron railings enclosing the recreation grounds were removed to help the war effort, as were the remainder of the railings and gates in Crossens, and three acres of the 'rec' were ploughed up for food production. Older scholars at St. John's were given extra holidays to help farmers with the harvest, particularly potato picking. C.H. Slater, the headmaster, sought to interest and involve his pupils in the rearing of rabbits for meat. In addition, the school gardens were used for the production of vegetables and excellent crops of broad beans and kidney beans were grown.

Day nurseries were provided during the war, principally to look after the children of mothers employed on war work. They were seen as a temporary war-time expedient and were administered by the Local Authority on behalf of the Ministry of Health. The Crossens War-Time Day Nursery was opened in October 1942 on a site in North Road, almost behind the Brockhouse plant. It was housed in an airy sectional building, with full-length windows. Day nurseries were open for much longer hours than schools, and the Crossens nursery opened at seven in the morning. It served breakfast and dinner; the children had a midday sleep; and a parent was charged a shilling (5p) a day. Trained, uniformed nurses staffed the nursery and the matron was Mrs. Moohan. The nursery catered for forty children between the ages of four months and five years. The first child to be enrolled was one-year-old Tony Gregory. In addition to the nursery there was still a welfare centre in Crossens catering for mothers and pre-school children. It was from this centre, in North Road, that concentrated orange juice and cod liver oil were distributed.

References

1. Gaham, J.W., *Seaport to Seaside* (1985), p.93.
2. Jarratt, J.E., *Municipal Recollections: Southport 1900-1930* (1932), p.36.
3. For a more complete account of the amalgamation see: Foster, Harry, *New Birkdale: The Growth of a Lancashire Seaside Suburb 1850-1912* (1995), pp. 20-25.
4. Bulpit, W.T., *Notes on Southport and District* (1908), p.85.
5. *S.V.*, 21 May 1908.
6. *S.V.*, 8 March 1956.
7. Knowles, A., *Auto Biography: My Forty Years of Motoring* (1970), p.14.
8. Botanic Gardens Museum (B.G.M.) *Recorded Reminiscences of the Vulcan*.
9. Knowles, A., p.13.
10. B.G.M.
11. *S.V.*, 9 August 1975.
12. *S.V.*, 15 July 1919.
13. *S.V.*, 5 June 1920.
14. *S.V.*, 19 August 1920.
15. *S.V.*, 25 January 1921.
16. S.R.L., Hales, D., *A History of Vulcan Cars 1899-1929* (1983), An unpublished, unpaginated typescript. This is not a history of the Company, but it does give a detailed account of the various models of Vulcan motor cars.
17. Knowles, A., p.13.
18. *S.V.*, 24 September 1921.
19. *Autocar* 16 October 1925.
20. Knowles, A., p.47.
21. *S.J.*, 27 June 1924.
22. *S.V.*, 6 May 1924.
23. *S.V.*, 28 February 1925.
24. *S.V.*, 20 February 1926.
25. *S.V.*, 25 September 1926.
26. *S.V.*, 18 January 1930.
27. *S.V.*, 18 February 1930.
28. Knowles, A., p.59.
29. *S.V.*, 6 February 1937.
30. Hales, D.
31. *S.V.*, 5 November 1927.
32. *S.J.*, 5 October 1923.
33. *S.V.*, 20 December 1924.
34. *S.V.*, 7 April 1979.
35. *S.V.*, 29 July 1933.
36. Croasdale, H., *St. John's C.of E. School Crossens* (n.d.), p.15.
37. *S.V.*, 22 October 1925.
38. *S.J.*, 11 May 1933.
39. Foster, Harry, *Don E Want Ony Srimps? The Story of the Fishermen of Southport and North Meols* (1998), pp.32-34.
40. *S.V.*, 12 February 1931.
41. Wareing, C., *Farming, Fishing, Football: Some More History and Memories of Banks Village* (n.d.), p.36.

42. *S.V.*, 24 September 1927.
43. *S.V.*, 29 July 1937.
44. *S.V.*, 20 June 1925.
45. *S.V.*, 31 July 1928.
46. *S.V.*, 30 July 1930.
47. Jarratt, J.E., p.47.
48. This section on housing is based on reports of proceedings of the Southport Town Council and on editorial comments and letters in the *S.V.*
49. *S.V.*, 20 December 1949.
50. *S.J.*, 28 September 1923.
51. *S.V.*, 30 July 1925.
52. Ormrod, M.E., reminiscences of a former teacher at St. John's
53. *S.V.*, 23 January 1923.
54. *S.V.*, 2 September 1924.
55. *S.V.*, 6 December 1924.
56. Edwards, Z., *The Vicar as Vagrant* (1910).
57. *S.V.*, 3 March 1927.
58. Walmsley, W.V. *St. John's Church, Crossens 1837-1937* (1937).
59. *S.V.*, 12 January 1924.
60. S.R.L., *Southport Education Committee Yearbooks* (1913 -1939).
61. Billington, J., *History of Crossens Rose Queen Festival* (1962), p.4.
62. *S.V.*, 14 September 1928.
63. *S.T.C. Minutes*, September 1940.
64. *S.V.*, 4 September 1981.
65. Knowles, A., *The Thoughts of a Machine Tool Setter* (n.d.).
66. Knowles, A., p.126.
67. *S.V.*, 3 February 1976.

CHAPTER FIVE

Farms and Factories Give Way to Housing 1945-2000

*Southport's attempts to attract industry to the town have been an
abysmal failure*
Witness at Public Enquiry in 1972

The Ribble Estuary

AFTER THE cessation of hostilities, Crossens became involved in an exotic municipal pipe dream. Blackpool Corporation wanted to develop Blackpool Airport, across the Ribble estuary at Squire's Gate, for major trans-Atlantic operations. It approached Southport Corporation about the possibility of linking its airfield with a sea-plane base at Crossens. It wanted to create a lagoon four miles long and fifteen feet deep in the Ribble estuary, with a tunnel and a road to give access. It was claimed that the scheme, which would cost £4,000,000, had the '... blessing of the Air Ministry' and the backing of private financiers. Blackpool wanted the support of the Southport Corporation to promote a parliamentary bill. No financial assistance was being sought from Southport. The Corporation, however, chose not to co-operate with its rival resort across the Ribble and continued to promote its own doomed scheme for a civic aerodrome at Kew.[1]

In the 1950s a vast new drainage scheme for Martin Mere was undertaken. It included building a new pumping station at Crossens, which cost over £1,000,000 and was the third largest in the country at the time. Three major waterways – Three Pools, Back Drain and the Sluice – converged on the pumping station *(Fig. 90)*. The improvements meant that it was finally possible to reliably control the water table on the Mere in relation to the agricultural needs. The pumping station was to serve a dual role '... primarily for land drainage, but during dry weather it maintains high water levels to alleviate lowland peat shrinkage.'[2] Princess Alexandra opened the scheme in

Fig. 90. New pumping station c.1963. The old pumping station can be seen in the background.
There was still a handful of small fishing boats operating from Crossens Pool

1961, but Crossens' pollution problems persisted. Heavy rainfall on the Mere led to the drainage channels being fouled by sewage. Chris Rigby, a schoolboy, writing in the Crossens Primary School newspaper, *Crossens Echo,* in 1962, reported that he had seen lots of dead fish floating on the water. He wrote: 'You almost needed a gas mask to get near to the pumping station. It's a good job it didn't smell like that when Princess Maria Alexandra was there.'[3]

In this intensively farmed area, one of the most serious forms of pollution is the run-off of pesticides and fertilisers into the drainage channels. After local government reorganisation in 1974, the North West Water Authority claimed to have inherited '... the worst polluted estuary in Great Britain.' Fine Jane's Brook and Crossens Pool were classified as 'grossly polluted'. At times of heavy rainfall Southport's sewage could flow into Fine Jane's Brook and the Three Pools waterway. There was serious pollution following storms in 1984 and 1987 when the fish stock was wiped out. Following a further leakage in 1991, North West Water paid £40,000 in damages for the pollution to the Hesketh Estate and the water had to be again re-stocked with fish. The catchment area is now the responsibility of the Environment Agency, which is adopting a multi-agency approach to its management. The Agency reported that the Crossens area '... used to be renowned for its prolific (coarse) fishery.'

Fig. 91. Bank End sewerage works. The old mill chimney can be seen in the background

Angling is still a major leisure activity and the major fish stock appears to be pike, roach, bream, tench, carp and perch.[4] Pike weighing up to twenty-four pounds have recently been caught.

Following the war, the ageing plant at the Bank End sewerage works was experiencing considerable difficulty in coping with increasing demand. On reaching the works the sewage had to be lifted by four large capacity gas-driven pumps in order for it to be passed through sedimentation tanks, filters and drying beds *(Fig. 91)*. Filtration was a natural process, with no chemicals being used. The vast quantity of sludge left as a residue was supplied to local farms. This plant was, however, completely inadequate to cope with post-war residential expansion in Southport, particularly the proposed housing development in Ainsdale. Periodically it also produced noxious smells. In the 1960s, the plant underwent a major updating, which increased its capacity. One unfulfilled plan for the new works envisaged that the electricity supply that it required could be generated by a system of 'sludge digestion'. Work on the new plant continued into the early 1970s. After its completion, the Town Clerk was able to declare that there was '... virtually a complete absence of smell from the works';[5] whilst George Barton, the plant manager, enthusiastically described how '... the treated effluent gushes all clear and sparkling under the scarlet tidal gate into Crossens Pool.'[6]

The effluent passing through the Bank End plant did not always represent the full extent of Southport's sewage. There were still overflow pipes running across the beach, which from time to time put untreated waste into the sea; whilst as we have seen it also escaped inland into Fine Jane's Brook. Later, new European standards, which were set to clean up bathing waters, meant that the *status quo* was no longer acceptable. North West Water came up with a £75,000,000 scheme for the town. Critical to this scheme was the building of a three-mile long interceptor sewer across the front of Southport, from Pleasureland to Crossens. The bore of the new sewer was some nine feet, and its depth below the surface was up to forty-five feet. It was built by a large mechanical mole, which excavated spoil and simultaneously laid sections of concrete pipe. Building started in 1993, and all the work was done underground, without disturbing the ground surface or the buildings under which the mole worked. The problem of moving Southport's waste across relatively flat land, which had taxed the Victorian engineers and their successors, had been solved. Not surprisingly, this tunnelling was responsible for about a third of the total cost of the scheme. The plant at Bank End had to be upgraded to cope with the increased volume of throughput. At the heart of the new high-tech treatment is a gigantic deep shaft biological plant. It is eighty-three metres deep, that is big enough to house fifteen double-decker buses piled one on top of the other. When it was built it was thought to be the biggest of its kind in the world. Nevertheless, it was soon necessary to increase the wastewater storage capacity of the plant. The proof of the pudding was in the eating, and despite occasional pollution caused by discharges further up the Ribble, Southport's beaches began to meet the required standards.

Small boats were still fishing commercially from Crossens into the 1960s. But as a result of the silting of the Pool Channel boats were repeatedly grounding, and by 1974 the last of the fishing boats had left Crossens. Two engineers working on the drainage improvement scheme in the late 1950s reported:

> The width of the foreshore is quite out of the ordinary, and low water mark on Spring Tides is nearly four miles outside the sea wall. The water discharge by the Crossens River meanders across the saltings, mud and sands, before finally discharging into the Pinfold Channel.[7]

Local boat shrimpers moved to Formby, the channel there being the nearest point to Southport where it shelves sharply enough to put a normal boat into the water. These shrimpers included Peter Larkins of Crossens and Eric

Sumner. Sumner, a former resident of Marshside, had two boats – 'Sea Nymph' and 'Ribble Queen' – moored in the Formby Channel.[8] He also had a shellfish-processing plant in a building behind the south end of Rufford Road.

In 1968, tipping of hard core had started on an extension of the coastal road to The Plough at Crossens. It then ran from Woodvale, at the south of the borough, to Marshside. The twenty-two and a half acres that were required for this extension were bought from the Trustees of the Naylor-Leyland Estate. When the extension, which cost some £80,000, was eventually opened in 1974, a large roundabout was constructed at The Plough, which entailed the demolition of the Scarisbrick bungalows. The new road allowed traffic to by-pass Crossens. The land, which had

Fig. 92. Brockhouse's Corgi motor cycle

been enclosed, between the coastal road and the old 1892 sea-wall provided marshy pasture for raising cattle. The marshland outside the road became an extensive nature reserve administered by English Nature. Wildfowlers were still able to shoot on these marshes, but only under the strictest controls.

Shrinking Industries

In the early post-war years, the Brockhouse factory at Crossens was still a substantial operation. Swords had been turned into ploughshares. The most striking example was the Corgi Motor Cycle; this machine was based on a folding motor cycle, which had been produced for army parachutists *(Fig. 92)*. A standard motor cycle – the Indian Brave – was also manufactured. In addition, President Tractors were assembled; there was a line for producing Venetian blind slats; and a line for producing cold rolled steel sections for prefabricated building. Interestingly, some of these sections were used in pre-fabricated housing in nearby Merlewood Avenue. A transition to peacetime products was not total, however. Several large automatic lathes continued to be used to produce 40mm shells for the army; there was a contract to make mine-sinker mechanisms for the navy; whilst other items were produced for the Air Ministry. Veterans from the days of the Vulcan Company were still employed at Crossens. They included Joe Hampson, the deputy-head of the tool room, who was related to the Company's founders. This group of pre-war employees still retained a strong nostalgic allegiance to Vulcan.

119

Fig. 93. Mullard's factory extensions c.1971. The major extension was alongside Balmoral Drive. The Bankfield Engineering and Raylor factories can be seen on the site of the former railway station yard, as can the caravan sales park

By 1949 Brockhouse was suffering from a declining order book, and the workforce had shrunk to 170 people working a four-day week. Early in 1950, ninety-seven dismissal notices were served. Initially, the Company claimed that they were mostly for clerks, inspectors and progress engineers, but a spokesman later told the *Southport Visiter* that: 'Many of the dismissed workers are to be replaced by machines.'[9] The strategy obviously did not work and the Company decided to rationalise the increasingly diverse business it ran from Crossens, closing some lines and redistributing others among its factories in the Midlands.

In 1955 Brockhouse leased the Crossens plant in two parts. The Church-town end went to the Magnetic Component Division of Mullard Blackburn. Mullard, which had been bought out by the Dutch electronic giant Philips in 1921, prospered with the boom in the television industry. Large illuminated signs on the clock tower proudly proclaimed the presence of the new tenant, and there was a strong air of optimism with the arrival of this 'modern' technology-based industry. The workforce rose to over 1,000 employees and further buildings were erected along the Balmoral Road frontage of the site. The new buildings included recreational facilities for the staff *(Fig. 93)*. A staff netball team reflected the fact that many of the workers in the factory were women. In the 1990s, despite opposition from the unions, changes in technology and competition resulted in some lines closing and others being transferred to countries where labour was cheaper. By the year 2000 only a skeleton staff remained on site in Crossens.

The Crossens end of the factory was to have a more chequered career, with periods when parts of the buildings were without tenants. In 1955 it was leased to Power Sampas (later to become International Computers and Tabulators Ltd.), a punchcard machine pioneer in computer development. Into the 1960s, this company was still actively recruiting skilled engineering workers. There appears to have been an active works' sports club and social club. Later tenants included Essex Wire (U.K.), which produced motor accessories. From 1968 The Book Centre, a company that employed about 140 workers to store and distribute books, was a tenant. Dorman Smith Traffic Products, which made safety lights for use on roadworks, followed; and more recently, space has been used by a plastics company – Plastics for Industry – and Bollards, a firm specialising in manufacturing exhibition stands.

Other small engineering businesses also located at Crossens. Alongside the railway, in the goods yard, were the workshops of the Bankfield Engineering Company, a firm specialising in sheet metal work and coach building. They occupied the old railway shed, and built an additional large shed for the repair and storage of industrial vehicles and buses. A 1951 survey put the workforce as being fifty strong. One well-remembered local contract was the building of a tram for the pier. Following the nationalisation of the railways in 1948, the *Beeching Report* of 1963 recommended massive rationalisation, including the closure of many local lines. Although 2,500,000 passengers a year were using the Southport to Preston line it became a victim of this purge, and in 1964 Crossens lost its railway *(Fig. 94)*. A section of the redundant track way was absorbed into the Mullard's site; whilst the old station site, including some buildings, became part of the small industrial estate. Raylors' engineering works was a major occupant. This business grew from the enterprise of a local ex-serviceman, Harold Taylor, who started by renovating old concrete mixers and had a small workshop in a corner of the Bankfield Engineering Company's shed. After taking a partner, who gave his name to the company, Raylors became a major national supplier of scaffolding. The Company received an enormous boost from its role in the development of the off-shore oil industry. Raylors later absorbed the premises of the defunct Bankfield Engineering Company. From 1969, part of the old railway yard was used for caravan sales, and later became a store and sales point for 'bottled' gas. There were also factories alongside the Brockhouse factory in Rufford Road. In

Fig. 94. Crossens station 1964 – This photograph was taken shortly before the closure

1951 Hartwood Hosiery employed some seventy-five people, mostly women, and in 1965 an extension was added to the factory. Another factory in this area was Presletta, which manufactured an internationally successful dry transfer lettering system, invented by Charles Revell of Coudray Road. The Ideal Laundry, in Brook Street, was still providing employment for more than fifty people, again mostly women, and it continued to operate into the 1960s, when the widespread introduction of domestic machines severely diminished this industry.

From the early 1950s, plans for an industrial estate based on Dock Lane featured in the Corporation's town planning schemes. One of the early prospective tenants was Mullards, which in 1954 negotiated for a twenty-eight acre site for an electronics factory, but did not proceed. The Corporation became involved in protracted negotiations with a London developer, and later sold forty-five acres of what were described as 'waste fen' to a holding company for just £500. Dock Lane was an old cobbled pathway between Crossens and Marshside and its name was changed to Fylde Road and the industrial estate became Cambridge Park. Lord Derby cut the first sod of this development in 1965. L.J. Brown, the chairman of the first company to build on the site, claimed that the low-level former marsh land had presented no problems for the construction of his engineering works.[10] What

Fig. 95. Two factory units on the Fylde Road fields c.1965

did present a problem was the refusal of the Board of Trade to allow Cambridge Park to be designated as part of the Merseyside Development Area, with its associated benefits for developers. Nevertheless, six units had been built by 1968, in which several hundred people were employed *(Fig. 95)*. Then, despite much advertising, development dried up.

One of the area's few industrial success stories occurred later alongside the new coastal road, just inland of Bank End sewerage works. Despite predictions that paper records would give way to electronically stored information, Frank Wilson (Filing) Limited had built up a successful business manufacturing paper storage systems. Their existing factory was located in the old tram sheds in Churchtown village. The Company, trading under the name of Railex, erected a large purpose-built factory at Crossens.

Suburban Developments

Like World War One, World War Two gave a boost to council house building. The government asked local authorities to have housing schemes in place for completion within two years of the cessation of hostilities in Europe. The demand for public housing put pressure on the outlying suburbs of Southport, where there were still areas of farmland within the borough. As early as March 1944, plans were passed for building 106 houses on an eleven-

Fig. 96. The Causeway Farm estate

acre plot at the rear of Causeway Farm, between the angle of Rufford Road and Preston New Road *(Fig. 96)*.[11] To compensate for this loss, James Caunce of Causeway Farm temporarily leased seven acres of the Preston New Road Recreation Ground, which still retained its wartime designation for agricultural use. The Corporation obtained a second six and a half-acre plot for sixty-six houses by compulsory purchase order in 1946, between Land Lane and New Lane. The plan was to build fifty three-bedroom houses and sixteen two-bedroom houses on this Drewitt Crescent site. The use of German prisoners of war to work on the project was considered and rejected. Drewitt Crescent was built up before the Causeway site, and the first houses were occupied in 1947 *(Fig. 97)*. Following the fashion of the time, Drewitt Crescent took its name from the chairman of the Estates Committee; whilst one of the roads on the Causeway Estate (Irvin Avenue) was named after a councillor serving on the Committee. Dawson Avenue was named after a retired Borough Treasurer. The Committee considered, but rejected, the possibility of giving direct access for vehicles from The Causeway onto busy Preston New Road, although a footpath was created.

In the early 1950s developers were given permission to build in Crossens' 'Lake District' – Holmdale Avenue and Asland Gardens. This scheme had been started in the 1930s, but the road had remained unmade and unlit.

Private developers, including Septimus Rostron, built on the stretch of vacant plots on Preston New Road, behind the Causeway Estate. By 1960 Crossens had a population of approximately 2,800 inhabitants.

Continuing pressure on building land within the Borough of Southport persuaded the Corporation to grant planning permission for Crowder-Barton to build an estate of some 150 houses – Skipton Avenue and Harrogate Way – in 1969. The estate was on Scorefield Pasture, a twenty-two acre triangle of low-lying reclaimed marsh between the new coastal road, which was screened by an earth bank, and the waters of Crossens Pool *(Fig. 98)*. The houses were protected from high water only by the built-up bank of Crossens Pool, which acted as a funnel for the incoming tide. Although providing an adequate sea defence in normal times, the earth bank was not able to cope with the combination of a very high tide backed by gale force wind, gusting up to ninety miles per hour, which drove the waters on shore in November 1977. The bank was breached and many of the houses were inundated. There were over two feet of floodwater in Ken Pike's house at 71 Harrogate Way. The residents were evacuated to The Plough, where landlord Albert Greere and his wife Jean provided hot drinks and food, and forty homeless families were accommodated overnight in Marshside Day Centre. Much of the rescue work was undertaken using tractors with trailers from nearby farms, but the wash they created exacerbated the conditions in the houses and a rowing boat was pressed into service. Ironically, adjoining Banks Road is the highest built-up spot in the borough, and residents looked down to see their neighbours sailing up Harrogate Way in a boat. Recrimination quickly followed the event. Crossens Flood Association was founded to look after the concerns of the families affected. Roy Baker, the vicar of Crossens, wrote to the local paper asking: 'What I would like to know, and what many people here would like to know, is how planning permission was ever given in the first place to build homes here. Historical records show what was likely to happen.'[12] The responsibility for giving permission plainly lay with the Corporation, but the advice given by North West Water and its role in the matter became a question of dispute. Despite some increase in the height of the bank, there was a later occasion when water came over without flooding the houses, and further improvements were made.

As has been indicated, industrial development on the Dock Lane/Fylde Road site was sluggish, and an agreement with the development company allowed residential building to the east of Fylde Road, at the Marshside

Fig. 97. Preparing the roads on the Drewitt Crescent site

Fig. 98. Building on the Skipton Avenue/Harrogate Way site 1969. The farms around Banks Road and The Plough were still much in evidence

126

end. The absence of potential industrial developers for the Crossens end meant that this area became the target for housing developers. One company had an application to build 300 bungalows turned down by the Council. The company appealed against this decision. A surveyor appearing on their behalf pointed to the '... abysmal failure of Southport's attempts to attract industry to the town.'[13] The Corporation still hoped that an administrative link with Merseyside might bring the benefits of Development Area status. Eventually, in 1972, this area – Cambridge Park Estate – was given over to housing. Unusually, some of these bungalows were built with the rear of their back gardens facing on to Preston New Road. One Councillor later admitted that this had been a mistake. The developers, Howard Estates and the Albert Brothers, successfully sought the alteration of the name Bank End Lane, with its connotations of the Bank End Sewerage Works, to the more attractive sounding Ferry Side Lane. The 1890s sea-wall provided an outer limit to the housing development. In 1974 Southport County Borough was absorbed into the Metropolitan Borough of Sefton, but this change did not materially effect the emerging pattern of development in Crossens.

The last half-century has seen the progressive filling of vacant plots by houses. In recent years the buildings and yards and surrounds of surviving farms in the village have given way to small estates of private housing *(Fig. 99)*. Albert Brothers received permission in 1979 to build eighty-nine houses on part of Plough Farm and Hey Farm on the south side of Water Lane. The old farmhouse of Hey Farm still adds welcome variety to this estate. Barton's Farm, opposite The Plough, was later demolished for a further estate. This development appears to restrict the possibility of a new road being built between Preston New Road and the A565 at Banks. It is interesting to recall that the *Development Plan for the County Borough of Southport 1952* gave the highest priority to such a road to replace the narrow winding Water Lane, which still survives as a flawed link. Residential infilling also took place along Banks Road.

Agriculture had not been entirely obliterated in Crossens. The occupants of the ribbon of new bungalows alongside Water Lane, built by Septimus Rostron, were enraged when, in 1971, they discovered a new 'giant storage barn' being built so close to their property that it completely obstructed the view. Much of the land down New Lane continued to be cultivated. In the early 1950s, the Naylor Leylands sold off their share of the holdings, which they had received from the Scarisbrick Trust in 1925. This included agricultural land in and around Crossens. Roger Fleetwood Hesketh of Meols

Fig. 99. Land for the builders c.1969 – Developers have since built on much of the farmland and on the sites of many of the farm buildings shown in this photograph. The tall building in the trees was the vicarage

Hall, the joint lord of the manor, bought some of the farms fringing the Mere, including New Midge Hall.

In 1960, the question of having an off-licence in the village became the subject of tension. The Plough, which urban change had placed on the fringe of the village, held the only drink licence in Crossens. Hugh Buller, a news-agent at no. 92 Rufford Road, applied for an off-licence. Despite objections from fifty-six Crossens residents the application, which was strongly supported by the vicar, the Rev. T.T. Williams, was successful.[14] As in other working-class suburbs of Southport, the introduction of supermarkets and shopping malls devastated the business of small neighbourhood shops. In 1972 Nyman's, the village's only chemist shop, closed, thus making Churchtown the nearest pharmacy. In Crossens many of the surplus retail units have been converted or replaced by domestic dwellings. More recently industrial units around the former station and alongside the old Vulcan factory have been developed as housing estates. After Raylors had been sold as a going concern the business was closed down. The industrial premises around the site of the old station were cleared, and in 2001 an application to build thirty-three two-storey houses on the property of Raylor Engineering's Station Works was successfully made. Will the old Vulcan site eventually follow in this process?

Religion, Schooling and Leisure

The Parish Church of St. John appears to have shared the post-war boom in community involvement. Under the leadership of the Rev. H.T. Rider, the Church had a thriving Mothers' Union, Men's Fellowship, Guild and Dramatic Club. The church accounts were sound and in 1950 the interior of the church was completely re-decorated. There was a vibrant youth club, with a Council of Youth, which ran a monthly dance. The large room over the Co-operative store was used for many activities, including dances. The club also participated in the town's Youth Drama Festival and Youth Eisteddford.

It seems that this level of activity at St. John's was not maintained and that the church suffered a period of neglect prior to the induction of the Rev. Roy Baker, a curate at St. Cuthbert's, as vicar in 1973. He immediately reported that the dilapidation in the church's structure was so severe that there was a danger that it would have to be closed.[15] The threat posed by loose plaster falling from the walls and ceilings limited the use of the building. Much of the woodwork was infested with beetles, and pigeons plagued the church. Their droppings had made the belfry unusable; in fact it was later estimated that ten and a half tons were removed. Sadly, the depredations of the pigeons were not restricted to the belfry, as the birds had also invaded the body of the church. Roy Baker described the church as a 'rotting hulk'. It had also suffered from vandalism. A chalice had been stolen from within the church and a teak garden seat from the grounds. When Baker took over, the Department of the Environment had already made a grant of £2,325, but this could only be used for the restoration of the grounds. An appeal was made and £17,500 was raised, and after restoration the church was re-hallowed in 1975, with a congregation of 600 in attendance. The church decided that the expense of restoring the belfry to a condition that would allow the peal of bells to be rung was too great, and that they preferred to prioritise the creation of a new parish centre. The members did, however, wish to retain the sound of bells in Crossens and favoured the much cheaper alternative of installing a cassette recording system. This was not a matter that could be resolved by the congregation. It required a decision of the Diocesan Consistory Court, which had to meet at Crossens. Despite considerable opposition from the traditional lobby in the diocese, the court eventually ruled in the church's favour. Then, in 1980, though the generosity of Sir Vivien Edward Naylor-Leyland, St. John's was able to acquire and refurbish the old Primitive

Methodist Chapel as a parish centre. In two years the parishioners had raised £9,000 towards an estimated cost of £16,000.

When the bell recording system was installed, the bells had been retained in the tower and following a successful appeal for funds they were later brought back into use, thus making St. John's one of the handful of churches in Southport with this facility. By 1990, the 104-year-old slate roof of the church was leaking and an appeal was launched to raise the £40,000 required for the necessary repairs.

It was not just the church building that had suffered from neglect. It appears that the Georgian vicarage was in an even worse condition (see Fig. 99). There was an alder tree growing through the lounge floor and a tawny owl living in the main bedroom.[16] The kitchen still had an old slop stone and a pump. It had been scheduled for demolition in 1940, and in 1950 the church authorities had unsuccessfully sought a building licence to replace it, at a time when licences were limited and priority was being given to the creation of further public housing. The resourceful Roy Baker, who like Bulpit had an interest in local history, later discovered that there was still '… glebe land in the parish.'[17] The last resident minister to farm it had been Cornwell in the 1860s. With the consent of the Queen and the Privy Council, this land was returned to the Liverpool Diocese and in return a new vicarage was built without any cost to the parish.

The last interment of a Scarisbrick in the family mausoleum was in 1967. Like the church, the mausoleum had suffered from neglect and vandalism, and estate workers effected repair and restoration work in 1979. In 1982 meddlers in black magic desecrated it, and this resulted in a service of exorcism being held.[18] Wanting to shed their responsibility for maintaining the building, the Scarisbrick Estate Trustees sought the permission of the Diocesan Consistory Court to demolish it, but the local Council made it a listed building. David Scarisbrick later told the *Southport Visiter* of a scheme to open the mausoleum for public interment to help fund its repair and maintenance.[19] The coffins of the embalmed bodies of the twelve members of the Scarisbrick family would be put into one of the transepts, leaving space for 500 solid oak cabinets for public interment at £500 a time. Scarisbrick claimed to have a firm of local undertakers willing to sell spaces and also to have the support of the vicar of St. John's. Some of the money raised would go to the parish. The scheme, which had the potential to raise £250,000, was never brought to fruition. The Scarisbrick Trustees put a £5,000 repair scheme in place and sealed the building.

As part of a continuing review of Methodist provision in Southport, the future of the Crossens church was considered. The most critical period was probably the early 1970s. In the event, at a time when so many other Methodist churches were being closed, the Crossens church was retained.

In 1950 St. John's School became a local education authority 'controlled' school. Although still an Anglican voluntary school, this category gave greater control to the local authority, and in return they accepted more of the financial burden than was the case with school that had 'aided' status. The long-awaited new secondary school to serve the north end of the Borough was finally opened in 1951. Originally designated Churchtown County Secondary (Modern) School, it took the name of Stanley, the family name of the opener Lord Derby. It was sited on reclaimed marshland at the end of Marshside Road. When it opened St. John's School finally lost all its eleven-plus pupils. Thereafter, they had to transfer to one of the secondary schools, according to the results of the eleven-plus examinations.

Although St. John's School had lost its older pupils, the increase in the size of the village and successive 'baby booms' put pressure on the accommodation. In the late 1960s, when J.R. Hartley was the headteacher, the school had a single-storey extension containing two classrooms. This was still insufficient to meet the increasing demand for places and the school absorbed the first-floor rooms of the now defunct Institute, and two further classrooms were created. The running of the Rose Queen Festival, which was in decline, had been taken over by the school during the mid 1950s.

With the end of the war day nurseries, which had allowed mothers to work in factories, were no longer a national priority. Crossens Day Nursery, in North Road, was closed in October 1946. The Corporation decided to purchase the building from the Ministry of Works for use as a nursery school. It paid £950 for the building and a further £250 to the landowner for the quarter-acre plot. Crossens Nursery School was opened in the September of 1947, with Miss Eveline Houghton as superintendent and one qualified assistant mistress.[20] Continuing to occupy the wartime building, the school has thrived under local education authority control, and still operates under the leadership of its head teacher Mrs. Gilbertson *(Fig. 100)*.

By 1964 local authority economies were having an impact on the village. The number of books issued annually from the Crossens Library was 60,000, well below the target figure of 100,000 and the opening hours were reduced from forty-five to twenty-four and a half hours a week, with the employment of only one assistant. Despite angry objections from local residents the authority decided to close the branch in 1980. Initially, planning permission

Fig. 100. Crossens Nursery School 2000 – still housed in the 1942 'temporary' building

Fig. 101. Crossens Library 2000 – closed and decaying

Fig. 102. St. John's Air Scouts – L to R Back row- John Broadhurst, Raymond Norbury, Harry Hosker, Peter Christian, John Ball, Roy Watkinson, Front row – Albert Bedford, Alan Wright, Denis Sutcliffe, Peter Ward (shouldered), John Todd, Bertie Harrison, Dave Gregson, George Ashcroft, Mike Keen, and John Rothwell

was obtained to convert the building into a sports changing room at a cost of £12,500. This would have been considerably cheaper than building a new facility for the recreation ground, but this project was shelved and dereliction has become the fate of the former library *(Fig. 101)*.

As in other suburbs of the town, the Boy Scout movement was strong in Crossens. The 40th St. John's was an Air Scout troop. These were comparatively rare, only having been introduced in 1941 *(Fig. 102)*. The scout masters – Bill Dobbins and John Halsall – were both teachers at the parish school. The 13th Southport Girl Guide Company continued to be active at St. John's; whilst the Methodist Church had the 2nd Southport Company of the Girls' Life Brigade and the 8th Southport Company of the Boys' Brigade attached to it. In 1976 the Girls' Life Brigade band became the only kilted band in the district, the kilts having been donated by a local businessman. In common with other working-class suburbs of Southport, during the early 1950s Crossens was to have its own Morris-dancing troupe. Under their leader, Maureen Jackson, it met in the Methodist schoolroom and the girls performed and competed at many local and regional events. Like other local troupes, the Crossens troupe had disappeared by the end of the 1960s.

Sports continued to flourish in Crossens. By 1953 Crossens Bowling Club had come into being and was using the green and the pavilion. Permission was later given to the club to erect a sectional hut, alongside the pavilion, for use as a clubhouse. Members were allowed to use it three evenings a week, after the recreation ground had closed.[21] Crossens Bowling Club now figures strongly in the local league. Crossens Football Club found a new home on Crossens Recreation Ground, and Crossens Cricket Club prospered. The post-war years saw the emergence of strong cricket teams that enjoyed success in the First and Reserve Division of the Southport and District League and in the Sandhurst Shield knockout competition. The 1949 final between Crossens and Rufford, which was played at the Rookery, attracted a crowd of over 1,500. The club was to win the shield and the league in this year. One of the club's most enthusiastic supporters was Harold Taylor of Raylors' Engineering. It was no coincidence that the sightscreens and score board were made from his firm's scaffolding, or that one of the bowlers worked for the company. The New Lane ground was on Fleetwood Hesketh land, and Roger Fleetwood Hesketh was the club president. This much-loved squire of North Meols regularly attended the Annual General Meeting and declared that there would always be cricket at New Lane whilst he was at Meols Hall. Commercial pressures meant that his son later demanded a more economic rent for the ground, and the club closed down in the early 1990s. The St. Phillip's team was briefly a tenant but it, too, was unable to afford to play at New Lane. St. Paul's, a founder member of the League in 1898, moved from Meols Park to the playing field at Bank End, in 1981. The club built a fully equipped pavilion and ran two senior teams and two junior teams. Sadly, the pavilion was regularly vandalised. Interestingly, the detached country villages around Southport have been able to maintain the social and sporting provision for youngsters that Crossens, now a residential suburb, has largely lost.

References

1. *S.V.*, 13 July 1944.
2. Environment Agency, *Local Environment Agency Plan Alt/Crossens Consultation Report,* (1999) p.8.
3. *Crossens Echo* (1962).
4. Environment Agency, pages 72 & 67.
5. Bayley-Brown, P.P., *Southport '71 Municipal Review* (1971).
6. *S.V.*, 10 February 1972.
7. Prus-Chasinski, T.M. & Harris, W.B., *River Crossens Major Improvement Scheme* (1958), p.3.
8. *S.V.*, 6 January 1970.
9. *S.V.*, 2 February 1950.
10. *Liverpool Echo*, 26 April 1968.
11. *Proceedings of the Southport Borough Council.* Information on council housing has been taken from the minutes of the Estates Committee, and on private development from the minutes of the Town Planning Committee.
12. *S.V.*, 19 November 1977.
13. *S.V.*, 8 January 1972.
14. *S.V.*, 6 February 1960.
15. *S.V.*, 27 March 1973.
16. *S.V.*, 3 May 1977.
17. *S.V.*, 28 April 1982.
18. *S.V.*, 28 April 1982.
19. *S.V.*, an undated cutting held by author.
20. *Minutes of the Southport Borough Council* – Education Committee.
21. *Minutes of the Southport Borough Council* – Parks and Cemeteries Committee.

CHAPTER SIX

Crossens:
Some Conclusions

O UR STORY started with Crossens as an agricultural hamlet in the
sparsely populated parish of North Meols. Its yeoman farmers enjoyed
the advantage of having much more fertile soil than was the case in
most of the remainder of this sandy parish. Unlike many of the other
inhabitants, who made a living from fishing, the residents of Crossens had a
bond with the land rather than the sea. The successful nineteenth-century
growth of Southport as a residential resort created a demand for building and
service workers, and many of Southport's poorest paid labourers lived in
Crossens. It was only in such outlying areas that the landowners would allow
the development of the cheap property that these labourers could afford to
rent. The labourers faced a long walk into town to their places of
employment. Although there was an increase in population, farming remained
the dominant activity in Crossens into the twentieth century.

On the surface, Southport's decision to absorb this poor, still largely
agricultural, detached northern neighbour into the buoyant urban borough
appeared to make little economic sense. In fact, there was a compelling reason
for Southport to seek such a move. The natural fall in the drainage of the area
was to the north, and Southport wished to secure access to the Ribble estuary
for the discharge of its growing volume of sewage. This would place the point
of discharge well away from, and down wind of its holiday beaches. After
amalgamation, the Southport Council was quick to develop the sewerage
works at Bank End, but was less enthusiastic in providing service facilities for
the village.

During the later years of the nineteenth century the vicar, the Rev. William
Bulpit, actively supported by Charles (later Sir Charles) Scarisbrick, his patron,
did much to improve social conditions and to establish a strong sense of
community and identity in his economically poor parish. Crossens was the
only area of Southport in which members of the Scarisbrick family were so

active. Encouraged by Bulpit, Charles Scarisbrick obviously regarded Crossens as 'his village' and personally paid for much of the development. Although later vicars, supported by members of the Scarisbrick families, and other benefactors, built on these foundations, the energy of the Bulpit/Charles Scarisbrick years was never recaptured.

The first decade of the twentieth century saw a dramatic development in Crossens – the arrival of the Vulcan motor works. Southport's only major factory, it was physically a most impressive building. Expansion came rapidly and the work force, many of whom lived in Crossens, was soon numbered in thousands. It had a tremendous impact on the community. Reminiscences from the families of former workers demonstrate the sense of pride that it engendered. It appears that it was no accident that the

'A Rufford Road Resident' – was the enigmatic title given to this Tomlinson slide

Vulcan years coincided with an upsurge in Crossens' confidence. Its Summer Festival emerged as the most successful community event in the area and the village's football and cricket clubs dominated the local sporting scene. Following the growth of the Vulcan, the local authority was to see Crossens as the natural location for further industrial development in Southport. In the event there was a limited take-up, but it was never on the scale envisaged.

Post World War Two efforts to encourage industrial and commercial development foundered on the reluctance of entrepreneurs to invest in this area, which did not enjoy the benefits of Merseyside Development Area status. Although cheap, reclaimed marshland was available, transport links were poor. Crossens was well removed from the motorway network and its railway line was closed in the 1960s. Meanwhile, the shortage of building land in other parts of the borough meant that developers looked to outlying Crossens. The gap between it and its neighbour Churchtown had already been closed. Vacant spaces within Crossens were filled; planning permission for houses on agricultural land was granted; land which had been designated for industry was released for housing; and finally former industrial sites were cleared for development. Crossens, the previously detached municipal Cinderella, took its place as another residential suburb of Southport. It has, however, its own fascinating and individual history, as this account clearly shows.

Sources

Archives

SOUTHPORT REFERENCE LIBRARY (S.R.L.)
Census Enumerators' Returns 1851,1861,1871,1881,1891,1901
Southport Town Council (S.T.C.) Proceedings
North Meols Parish Vestry (N.M.P.) Proceedings (mss.)
Southport Education Committee Yearbooks (1913-1939)
Directories – various
The Cheetham Papers
The Glasgow Papers
A Farm Lease granted by Robert Hesketh to Richard Wright (1754)
Articles to be observed by the members of The Cow Club, Crossens (1858)
Farming in Southport: Recollections of Robert Seddon (2002)

BOTANIC GARDENS MUSEUM (B.G.M.)
Recorded Reminiscences of the Vulcan
Photographs of the Vulcan

PUBLIC RECORD OFFICE, LONDON (P.R.O.)
Educational Files – North Meols
Ed. 7/67 *Preliminary Statements*
Ed. 16/187 *Local Education Authority Supply File*
Ed. 21/100 *Public Elementary School Files*

NATIONAL SOCIETY, LONDON (N.S.)
St. John's C.E. School – Letter File

ST. JOHN'S C.E. SCHOOL, CROSSENS
Log Books (L.B.) Mixed 1892-1918
            Infants 1898-1918

PRIVATELY HELD
An Insurance Claim Form for Peter Rymer 1749
St. John's C.E. School Log Book Mixed 1863-1878
Vulcan memorabilia
Fred Holder's Journals six bound volumes (mss.)

Official Reports

Schools' Inquiry Commission (1867–8)
Local Environment Agency Plan Alt/Crossens Consultation Report (1999)

Newspapers

Southport Guardian (S.G.)
Southport Journal (S.J.)
Southport Daily News and West Lancashire Chronicle (S.N.) – (This newspaper regularly made
   changes to its title, but Southport Daily News was a constant)
Southport Visiter (S.V.)
Crossens Echo 1962 (S.R.L.)
Lytham and St. Annes Express 26 July 1935

Books

Addy, S.O., *The Evolution of the English House* (1898).
Ashton, W., *The Evolution of a Coastline* (1920).
Aughton, P., *North Meols and Southport: A History* (1988).
Barron, J., *A History of Ribble Navigation* (1938).
Bagley, J.J. (ed.), *The Great Diurnal of Nicholas Blundell of Little Crosby, Lancashire* (1970).
Bagley, J.J. & Hodgkiss, A.G., *Lancashire: A History of the County Palatinate in Early Maps*
   (1985).
Bailey, F.A., *A History of Southport* (1955).
Baines, E., *History of the County Palatine and Duchy of Lancaster* (1870 edition).
Bland, E., *Annals of Southport and District* (1903).
Bracewell, W.A. (ed.), *Southport N.A.H.T. Conference Souvenir* (1935).
British Association, *Southport – A Handbook of the Town* (1903).
Bulpit, W.T., *Notes on Southport and District* (1908).
Camden, W., *Camden's Britannia 1697* (Facsimile edition 1971).
Cannadine, D., *Patricians, power and politics in nineteenth-century towns* (1982).
Clare, R.L., *A Short History of North Meols* (1952).
Clarke, M., *The Leeds and Liverpool Canal* (1990).
Cotterall, J., *How Southport got its Churches* (1992).
Curtis, Bill, *The Golden Dream: The Biography of Sir Peter Hesketh Fleetwood, Bart., and the
   founding of the town of Fleetwood in Lancashire* (1995).
Farrer, W., *A History of the Parish of North Meols* (1903).
Foster, Harry, *New Birkdale: The Growth of a Lancashire Seaside Suburb* (1955).
Foster, Harry, *Don E Wont Ony Srimps? The Story of the Fishermen of Southport and North Meols*
   (1998).
Gaham, J.W., *Seaport to Seaside* (1985).
Hall, E. (ed.), *Miss Weeton: Journal of a Governess 1811-1825* (1939).
Harrop, Sylvia, *Old Birkdale and Ainsdale: Life on the south-west Lancashire Coast 1600-1851*
   (1985).
Howard, R.B., *The Aughtons of Aughton and North Meols* (1997).
Jarratt, J.E., *Municipal Recollections: Southport 1900-1930* (1932).

Knowles, A., *Auto Biography: My Forty Years of Motoring* (1970).

Lloyd, L., *Southport and North Meols Fishermen and Boat Builders* (1998).

Mutch, A., *Rural Life in S.W. Lancashire 1840-1914* (1988).

Pevsner, N., *The Buildings of England: North Lancashire* (1969).

Robinson, F.W., *A Descriptive History of Southport* (1848).

Thompson Watkin, W., *Roman Lancashire* (1883).

Sumner, J., *A Guide to Southport* (1849).

Walmsley, W.V., *St.John's Church, Crossens 1837-1937* (1937).

Wareing, C., *Farming, Fishing, Football: Some More Memories of Banks Village* (n.d.).

Whittingham, T.E., *Around 450 not out* (1985).

Wilkinson, J. (ed.), *The Letters of Thomas Langton, Flax Merchant of Kirkham 1771-1781* (1994).

Wright, G., *Southport 200 Years Ago* (1992).

Theses, Articles, Monographs, and Pamphlets

Baker, R., *Crossens: What's in a Name?* (n.d. typescript S.R.L.).

Billington, J., *History of Crossens Rose Queen Festival* (1962 S.R.L.).

Bray, D.L., 'Jobs and Jobbers in Mid-Victorian North Meols', *North Meols Family History Society Journal*, Spring 1992.

Cheetham, F.H., 'The Records of the Court Baron of North Meols 1640-1643', *T.H.S.L.C.* vol. 34, 1932.

Coney, A., 'Fish, fowl and fen; landscape and economy on seventeenth century Martin Mere', *Landscape History* Vol. 14, 1992.

Croasdale, H., *St. John's C.of E. School, Crossens* (n.d. typescript S.R.L.).

Edwards, Z., *The Vicar as Vagrant* (1910).

Foster, H.J., *The Influence of Socio-Economic, Spatial, and Demographic Factors on the Development of Schooling in a Nineteenth Century Lancashire Residential Town* (M.Ed. 1976 S.R.L.).

Garlick, A., *A Miller's Journal by Joseph Leadbetter 1824-1905* (1999 typescript S.R.L.).

Hales, D., *A History of Vulcan Cars 1899-1929* (1983 typescript S.R.L.).

Hosker, A., *The Fishing Industry of North Meols* (1953 typescript S.R.L.).

Knowles, A., *The Thoughts of a Machine Tool Setter* (n.d.).

Lloyd, R., *No Rehearsals, No Regrets* (1965 typescript S.R.L.).

Prus–Chasinski, T.M. & Harris, W.B., *River Crossens Major Improvement Scheme* (1958 S.R.L.).

Raines, F.R., 'Notitia Cestriensis or Historic Notices of the Diocese of Chester by R.R. Francis Gastrell D.D.', *Chetham Society*, vol. XXI, vol. II, 1850.

Rideout, E.H., 'Poor Law Administration in North Meols in the Eighteenth Century', *T.H.S.L.C.*, vol. 81, 1929.

Rimmington, R.T., 'Methodism and Society in Leicester 1881-1914', *The Local Historian*, May 2000, Vol.30, No.2.

Rogers, G., 'Lancashire Landowners and the Great Agricultural Depression', *Northern History*, 1968, vol. XXII.

Watkinson, J., 'A Retrospect' in *Crossens United Methodist Free Church May Fair and Grand Bazaar Handbook 1904*.

Whitehead, J., *Recollections of Southport Fifty Years Ago* (1894 S.R.L.).

Index of Names

ABRAM 12

Ainscough 12, 21, 56
  Hugh 94
  Thomas 68

Alexander, William 32, 38

Alexandra, Princess 116

Allonson 9

Ashcroft, George 133

Aughton 12, 21, 36, 56
  John 12, 37
  Jos 94

BAKER, Rev. Roy 125, 129, 130

Ball 8, 21, 54
  Gilbert 56
  G.H. 101
  John **71,** 72, 94, **133**

Bannester 9

Barron, Dr. 46
  Thomas 27

Barry, Dr. 65

Barton 12, 32
  George 115

Baxendale 21, 56
  John 27, 33
  Thomas 60

Bedford, Albert **133**

Benson, Mary 19

Birchley, W.R. 86

Bithell, Bill 109

Blevin (Blevine) 9
  Thomas 9

Blundell 9, 21, 56, 59
  Ellen 33, 54
  Henry 34

James 4
John 34
  Kenneth 105
  William 54

Blyth, Roger de 6

Bold 12, **13**

Bold-Hoghton, Sir Henry 22, 37

Bond (Bonnde, Boond) 7, 8, 12, 59
  Arthur 109
  Fred 54
  George 9
  John 109
  Thomas 54
  William 54

Booth, Tom 96

Brade, Richard 56

Bradshaw 9

Breakhill (Breakhell, Brekhill, Brekhyll,
  Brekyll) 9

Broadhurst, John **133**

Brookfield 7, 12, 21, 56, 104
  James 27, 72
  Moses 72
  Peter 15
  Robert 10
  Thomas 2

Brown, L.J. 122

Buller, Hugh 128

Bulpit, Rev. William 2, 3, 15, **16**, 50, **52,**
  53, 60, 62, **64,** 80, 104, 130, 135

Burnley, Miss 106

Burton, J.H. 62

CAUNCE, James 124

Chadwick 21, 56

Chew, William 30
Christian, Peter **133**
Coalbank, Susan 62
Connon, J.W. 62
Copeland 9, 12
Cornwell, Rev. William 42
Cotterall, Isaac 31, 74
Coudray 12
Critchley, Bessie 109
Cropper 12, 21, 56, 59
  Elsie 106
  Paul 94
  Thomas 94

DERBY, Lord 122, 131
Dixon, George 95
Dobbins, Bill 133

EASTHAM, Richard 74
Edwards, Rev. Z. 104
Evason, Albert 110

FLEETWOOD, Thomas 13, **14**
Forbes, William 97
Ford, Rev. Gilbert 38
Foster, James 29
  John 29
French, Matthew 7

GILBERTSON, Mrs. 131
Gildart, (Gildert) 21, 56
  William 68
Gordon, Billy 85
Greatbatch, George 32
Greere, Albert 125
Gregory, Tony 112
Gregson 12, 21, 23, 56, 59
  David 112, **133**
  Ellen 65
  Hugh 112
  Jane 9
  Richard 94

HALL, Edward Pardoe 97
Halsall 12
  John **133**

Hampson, Joseph 81, 89, 119
  Thomas 81, 84, 85, 88, 92
Harrison, Bert **133**
Hartley, J.R. 131
Haworth 9
Heaworth 9
Henrey, Rev. Thomas 42
Hesketh 12, 21, 30, 56, 63
  Rev. Charles 4, 22, 38
  Charles Bibby Fleetwood 104
  John 54
  Sir Peter Fleetwood 22, 25, 37, 40
  Robert 10
  Sir Roger Fleetwood 127, 134
Hibbott, G.H. 93, 99
Hodgson, John 101
Holden, Edward 50
Holmes, Richard 27
Hosker 21, 56
  Harry **133**
  Thomas **54**
Houghton, Eveline 131
Howard 21, 56, 59
  David 94
  John 55
  Percy 11
  Thomas 94

JACKSON 12, 59
  Maureen 131
Jaegar, Bill 110
Johnson 21, 56, 59
  Henry 72
  James 20, 104
  Tom 106
Jump, Sarah 60

KEEN, Mike **133**
Kitchen, Barnaby 12
Knowles, Arthur 110
  Ernie 85

LANGDEN, William **72**, 74, 94
Langton, Thomas 3
Lapes, Major J.E. 111

Larcombe, Rev. W.M. 98, 104
Larkin, Peter 118
Latham, Robert 76, 77
Leadbetter, Joseph 35
Leatherbarrow, William 33, 54, **63**,
Linaker (Liniker) 9, 12, 21, 56
   John 33
Lunn, James 50
Lyverpull, John de 6

MARSHALL, Robert 105
Mallett, Sophia 55
Matthews 9
Mayor, William 72, 74, 94
Molyneux, Henry 30
   James 30
Moohan, Miss 112

NAYLOR-LEYLAND, Sir Thomas 104
   Sir Vivien 127, 129
Neale, Edward 60, 94
Norbury, Raymond **133**

ORMROD, M.E. (Peggy) 103

PALMER, Dick **72**
Parkinson, John 34
Peet 21, 56
   James 27
Pike, Ken 125
Pilling, 109
Powsey, Prof. Bert 80
Pye, Thomas 56

RALPHS, Cyril 88
Ratcliffe 14
Rawstorne, Robert 76, 77
Raynor, Dr. C.G.J. 102
Revell, Charles 122
Rhodes, Len 84
Rigby, Chris 116
Rider, Rev. H.T. 128
Riding, John 68
Rimmer (Rimer) 9, 21, 59, 106
   Annie 55

Barnaby 94
Richard 95
Thomas 55, 83, 94
William 33, 86
Rostron, Septimus 125, 127
Rothwell, John **133**
Ryding 12
Rymer 9, 21, 56
   Peter 10
   Robert 43
   Thomas 9

SAWBRIDGE, Jack 111
Scarisbrick 9, 21, 22, 93, 105, 135
   Charles 2, 21, 22, 23, 29, 30, 35
   Sir Charles 23, **53**, 56, 60, 62, 63, **64**,
      65, 69, 74, 103, 105, 135
   David 130
   Sir Everard 104
   Mary Ann 23, 104
   William 23
   Thomas Eccleston 13, 14, 29
   Sir Thomas Talbot 63, **64**, 103, 104
Seddon, Robert 23, 74
Slater, C. H. 112
Smith, Walter 50
Sockett, William 54
Strange, Thomas 12
Such, Richard 9
Sumner, Eric 119
Sutcliffe, Denis **133**
Sutton 21, 56
   Cicely 34
   James 94
   John 95
   Richard 34
   William 9, 34

TAYLOR, Harold 121, 134
Tidmarsh 19
Timperley, William 50
Todd, John **133**
Tomason 9
Tomlinson 21, 56
   Elizabeth **101**, 102

Henry **36**, 55, 59, 102
Jane **102**
John 31, 34, **35**, 55, 102
Richard **72**, 74

WALL, George 111
Walmsley, Rev. W.V. 104, 105
Ward, Peter **133**
Wareing 8, 21, 56, 59
  James 94
  Jennie 105
  Robert 66
  Thomas 54
Watkinson 21, 56
  Agnes 106
  Henry 33
  James 54, 66
  Nanny 33
  Richard 44
  Thomas 42, 43

Weeton, Miss 19
Wignall 9
Williams, Rev. T.T. 128
Wilson, Frank 123
  Richard 55
Wood, Peter 60
Wright 8, 9, 12, 21, 56
  Alan **133**
  John 35
  Miles 66
  Nicholas 102
  Peter 4
  Richard 10, 76
  Thomas 66, 94
Wrigley, James Hardy 40

Index of Subjects

ASLAND Gardens 124

BANK End 80, 118, 123, 127, 134
Bankfield Eng. 121
Bankfield Lane 5, 21, 29, 33, 50, 103
Banks 25, 38, 49
Banks Road **2**
blacksmith 27, **31,** 72
boat-building 8, **76**
Book Centre 121
boulder clay **4**, 5, 20
Brade Street 54, 56, 99
Brockhouse Eng. 110, 111, 119
Brook Street 101

CAMBRIDGE Park 122, **123**, 137
carters 29
cordwainer (shoemaker) 34, 55
cottages 9, **10, 11, 12**, **20**, 21, **102**
coursing 37, 74
Crescent 99
cricket clubs 109, 134
Crossens
   Burial Club **67**, 68
   Club 68
   Cow Club 23, **24**, 34
   cross 1
   Drainage Board 96
   etymology 1, 19
   Festival 105, **106, 107, 108**, 131
   Incorporation 48
   Moss 23
   Pool 29, 44, 46, 49, 51, 70, 80, 96, 125
curling 73, **74**
Cylinder Bridge 29, 44

DAWSON Avenue 124
Dock Lane 25, 102, 122, 125
Dorman Smith 119
Douglas Navigation 15, 17
Drewitt Crescent 124, **126**

EELS 14, **15**
Essex Wire 121

FAMILY names 7, 8, 9, 12, 21, 56
farming 8, 23, 24, 27, **28**, 29, 30, 31, 68, **70**, 94, **95**
Ferry Side Lane 127
Fiddler's Ferry 7, 13
fishing 14, **15**, 37, 62, 74,, **75**, 95, **96**, 116, 118
Fold 21, **99**
football clubs 108, 109, 133

GAMEKEEPERS **35**, **72**, **73**, 74, 94
glebe land 40, 42, 130

HAND-LOOM weaving 32, 33
Harrogate Way 125, **126**
Hartwood Hosiery 122
Hearth Tax 9
Holmdale Avenue 101, 124
Home Guard 111

IDEAL Laundry 92, 93
inns/ public houses
   The Black Bull 33
   The Boot and Shoe 34, 59
   The Letter and Board 9
   The Plough 9, 21, 23, 31, 33, 34, 55, **58**, 59, 97, 102, 119, 125, 127

LAND Lane 21, 54, 101, 124
landowners 12,13, 21, 22, 103, 104
Leeds and Liverpool Canal 15
library (reading room) 110, 131, **132**
lime kiln 9
Liverpool House 9
lodging house 35
logboat 15, **16**

MARSHSIDE 25, 37, 38, 102, 125
Martin Mere 5, 7, 12, 13, 14, 15, 17, 19,
    22, 27, 49, 115
Methodist Church 130
    Primitive **43**, 44, 66, 105, 130
    United Free 42, 43, 44, 66, **67**, 105
mill 30
Mullards 120, **121**, 122
mussel bed 7

NEW Lane 55, 97, 124, 127
North Meols
    Bay 7
    Grammar School 9
    Parish Vestry 44, 45
    rectory 6, 7, 38
North Road **20**, 99, **100**, 101
nursery school 112, 131, **132**

PEAT 11
pigs 24, **25**, 52
Power-Sampas (I.C.T.) 121
Presletta 122
Preston New Road 102, 103, 125
pumping station/ mill **30**, 69, **70**, **116**

QUAY Nook 76, **96**

RAILEX 123
railway 50, 79, 121, **122**
Raylors **120**, 121, 128, 134
recreation ground 109, 110, 123, **124**, 133

residential development
    council 98, 99, **100**, 123, **124, 126**
    private 56, **58**, **59**, **60**, 61, 125, **126**,
      127, **128**
Ribble crossing 1, 2, 3, 4
    estuary 13, 22, 115
    Avenue 99, **100**
Roman hoard 2
Roselea Drive 101
Rufford Road 5, **20**, 21, **54**, 55, 56, **59**,
    60, **61**, **67**, **77**, **97**, **98**, 101,102, 128,
    129

ST. CUTHBERT'S Church 7, **8**, 41
St. John's Church 19, 40, 41, **62**, **64**, **66**,
    104, 128
    Institute **59**, 102
    School **39**, 40, 41, **59**, 60, 63, 65, 68,
      103, 105, 130, 131
Sawley Abbey 5
Scarisbrick Estate 22, 23, 55, 69, 103, 104,
    127, 129
    Mausoleum 65, **66**, 105, 130
sea-banks 9, 25, 26, 69, 102, 127
sea-salt 5
sewerage scheme 50, 51, 80, **117**, 118,
Skipton Avenue 125, **126**
Sluice 12, 29

TAILORS 34
threshing machines **71**, 72
Vulcan 81-92
    aeroplanes 86-87
    buses 91-92
    cars 84-91
    lorries 86-89

WATER Lane 45, **57**, 127
wells 11, 20, 52
wheelwrights 27
wildfowling 15, 119
windmill 9

Crossens

*Extract from 6"
Ordnance Survey
Map (1911)*

Crossens